Table of Contents

MATH   Page

How Big Is It? 2
Your child will learn all about size words and measuring.

Understanding Numbers 1-20 33
These pages will help your child learn to count to 20 and practice putting numbers
in the right order.

Fun With Math 65
Hidden pictures, riddles, and puzzles will help your child practice putting numbers
in the right order, recognize shapes, put puzzles together, and start to add.

What Time Is It? 97
Matching, cut-and-paste, and dot-to-dots will help your child learn to tell time
to the half-hour.

Kindergarten Math 129
Coloring, matching, and dot-to-dots will give your child lots of practice in the key
kindergarten math skills.

LANGUAGE

Manuscript Writing 161
Tracing, coloring, and other activities help your child practice pencil-and-paper skills
that are important steps in becoming an ABC expert.

Beginning Sounds 193
Phonics are fun with so many coloring, writing, matching, and word
completion activities.

Long Vowels 225
Your child can really begin to learn to read by practicing long vowel sounds through
short stories, word and picture matching, and dot-to-dots.

Short Vowels 257
These pages give your child lots of much-needed practice in listening for those
short vowel sounds that are the key to reading many first words.

Kindergarten Language 289
Tracing, matching, practicing alphabet order, and using scissors will help your child
master the major kindergarten language skills.

Parents: It is important for your child to be able to make comparisons. Use the ideas below to help him/her learn to see differences and to describe those differences.

What Size Is It?

Let's Talk
Find times to use the following pairs of words in conversations with your child.

big - little	**large - small**	**wide - narrow**
long - short	**tall - short**	**thick - thin**

For example:
"I want a thin piece of cake."
"Please, can you hand me that long pencil?"
"Who is bigger - you or your brother?"
"Stand by that tall tree so I can take your picture."
"Look at those small kittens."

Find It
Show three or more objects to your child. Say "Find the longest one.", "Give me the shortest one.", etc. Start with big differences working toward smaller ones.

Make a Book
Staple together sheets of paper. Write a title on the first page to serve as the cover of the book. Have your child cut pictures out of magazines that are the size word used on the cover. Paste, glue, or tape the pictures to the pages.

Parents: Point to each picture and have your child name it, then ask "Is it big or is it little?" before he/she begins the coloring activity.

Big or Little

Color **big** things.   ## X **little** things.

Parents: Point to each picture and have your child name it, then ask "Is it large or is it small?" before he/she begins the coloring activity.

Large or Small

Color **large** things.   **X small** things.

Circle the picture that is...

big

little

large

small

Draw a Picture

Draw a big ball.	Draw a little ball.
Draw a large animal.	Draw a small animal.

Comparing sizes

Parents: Point to each picture and have your child name it, then ask "Is it long or is it short?" before he/she begins the coloring activity.

Long or Short

Color long things red.   **Color short things green.**

Parents: Point to each picture and have your child name it, then ask "Is it tall or is it short?" before he/she begins the coloring activity.

Tall or Short

Color the tall ones.

　　　　　　　　　Comparing sizes

Parents: Read the directions to your child.

Color.

long — red

short — blue

Comparing length

Parents: Read the directions to your child.

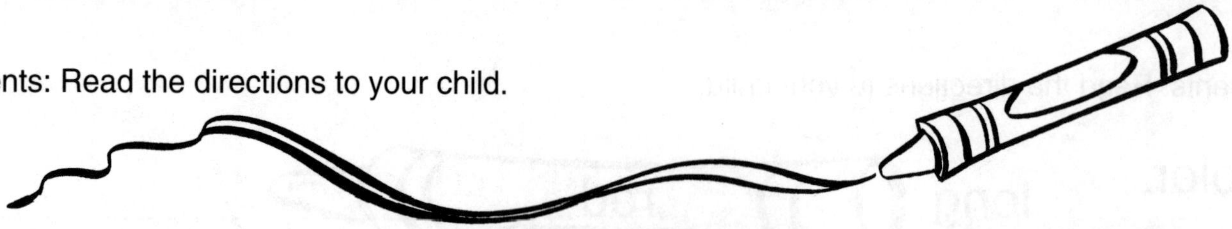

Draw a tall tree.

Draw a short flower.

Draw a tall giant.

Draw a short child.

Parents: Read the directions to your child.

Long or Tall

Put X on **tall** things.
Circle **long** things.

Comparing sizes

11

Parents: Read the directions to your child.

Which Is It?

tall

short

_____

- - - - - - - - - - - - - - - -   - - - - - - - - - - - - - - - -

_____

- - - - - - - - - - - - - -   - - - - - - - - - - - - - - -

_____

Comparing sizes; writing size words

Parents: Read the directions to your child.

What Size Is It?

big

little

Comparing sizes; writing size words

Parents: At this age your child needs to understand what happens when something is measured. He/she does not need to be using rulers and other measuring devices for a while. The activities on pages 14-28 will help develop this understanding. The activities use what is called non-standard measurement.

Measure the 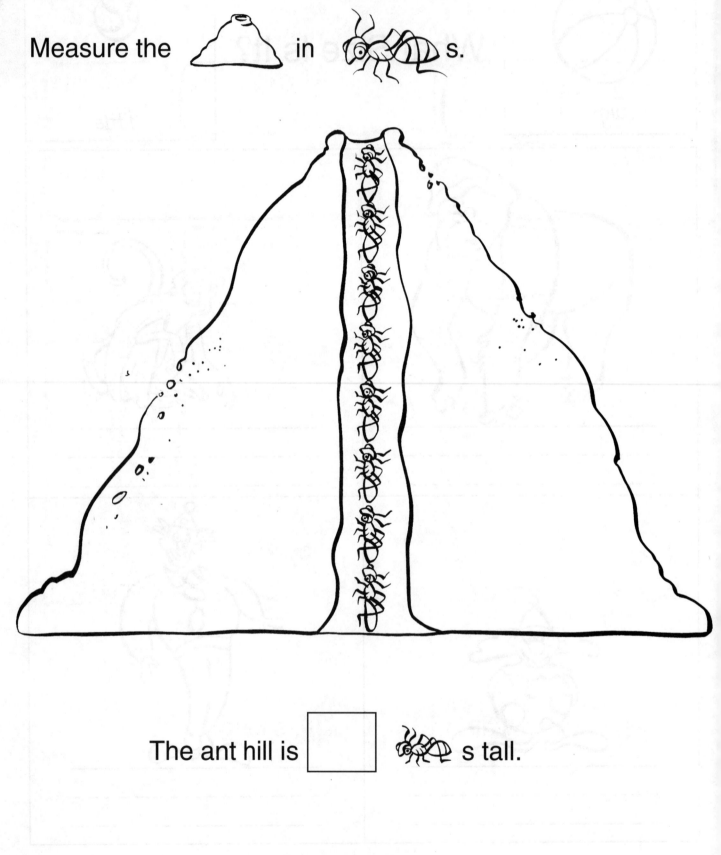 in s.

The ant hill is ☐ s tall.

Measuring

Measure the in  s.

The wall is  s long.

Measure the 🧷🧷 in 🐦s.

The clothesline is  ⬜ 🐦s long.

Measuring

Parents: Follow the directions below with your child.

Use Your Foot

Explain to your child that he/she is going to measure real things using his/her own foot. Go outside with your child and measure objects around the yard, garage, and house. You might measure things such as:

- the width of the front door
- the length of the sidewalk
- the width of the garage
- how far it is across the lawn

Have your child place one foot in front of the other in a heel-toe manner to make the measurement. Ask "How many feet was it from _____ to _____?"

Measure the same distance with your feet. Compare the difference. Ask "Why did it take more of your feet than mine?" *(You probably have bigger feet than your child, so it takes fewer of them to measure the same distance.)*

Measuring

Trace Your Foot

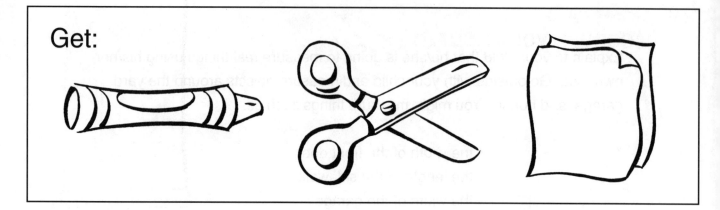

Get:

1. Put your foot on the paper.

   Trace it.

2. Make a lot of feet.

3. Put the feet in a row.

4. How many feet did you make?

   I made ⬚ feet.

Parents: Explain to your child that he/she is going to measure things using the feet he/she made. The feet need to be laid heel-to-toe along whatever is being measured.

How Many Feet?

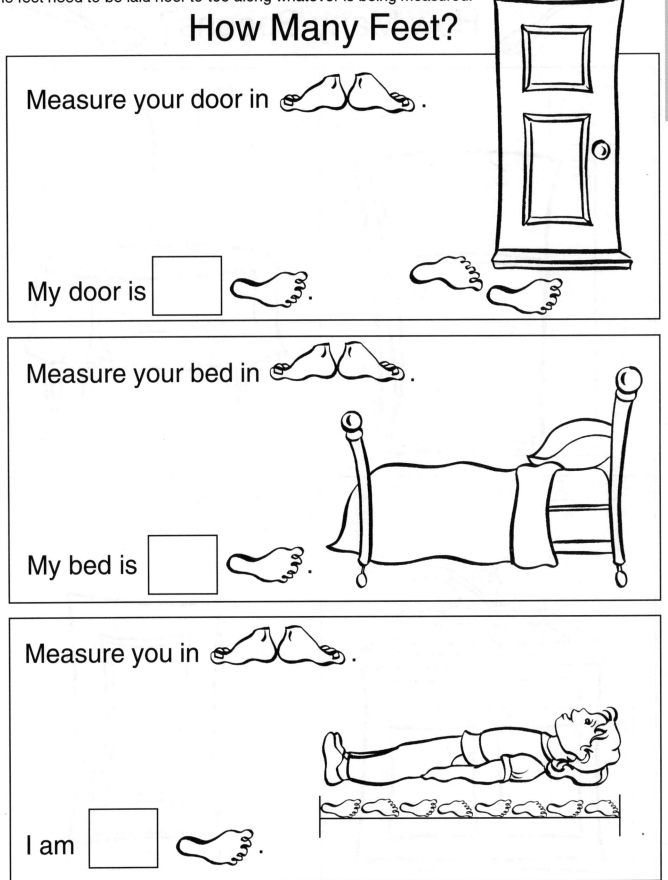

Measure your door in .

My door is [   ] .

Measure your bed in .

My bed is [   ] .

Measure you in .

I am [   ] .

Parents: Explain to your child that he/she is going to use a big spoon to measure things in the kitchen.

How Many Spoons?

Parents: Explain to your child that he/she is going to be measuring pictures with small counters. You will need to provide coins for page 21, and beans for page 22. Show your child how to lay the counters along the picture being sure they are end to end.

Measuring with Coins

Measuring with Beans

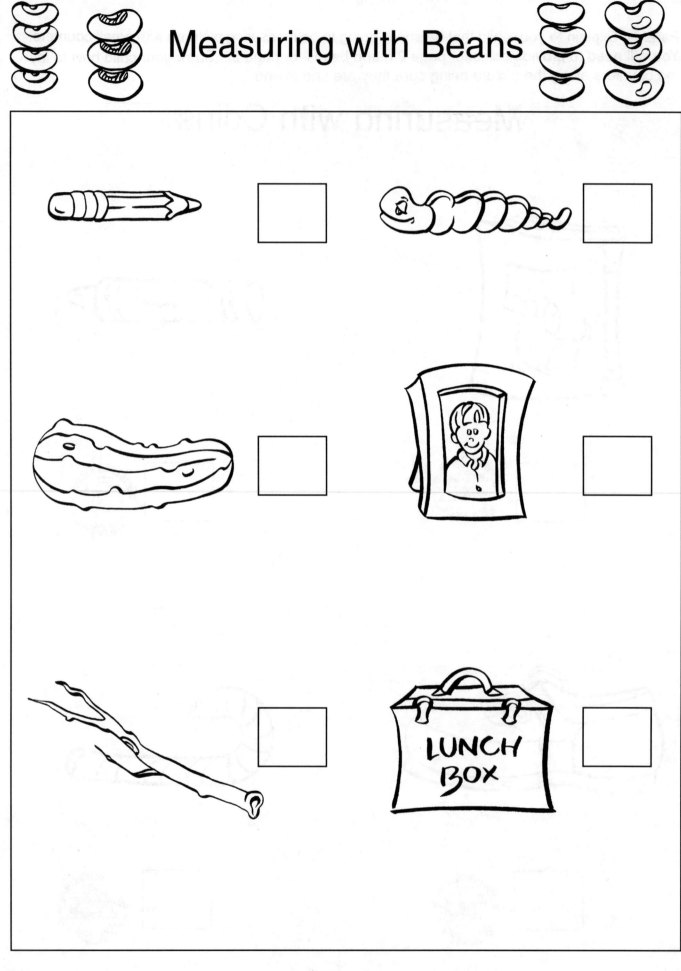

Parents: Explain to your child what he/she is to do on this page. Have your child cut out the bones at the bottom of the page to use as a measuring tool. Lay the bones end to end and count.

Measure the Dog House

How many bones long it it?

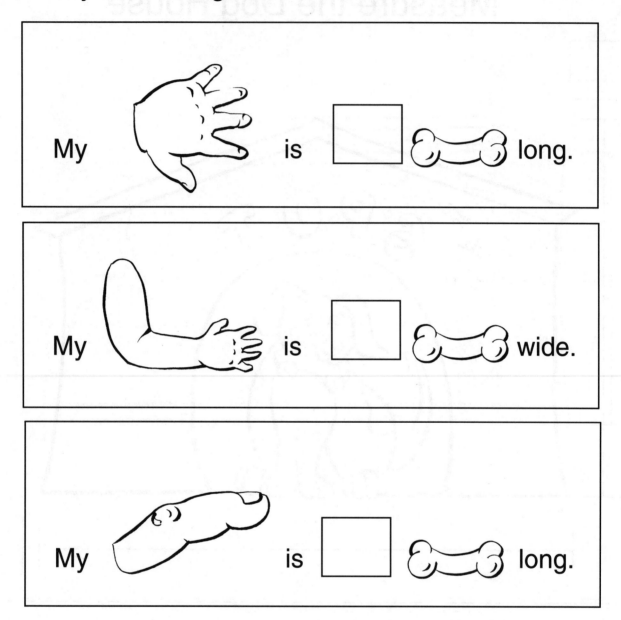

My (hand) is ☐ 🦴 long.

My (arm) is ☐ 🦴 wide.

My (finger) is ☐ 🦴 long.

Parents: Explain to your child what he/she is to do on this page. Have your child cut out the fish at the bottom of the page to use as a measuring tool. You may also use fish shaped crackers.

Measure the Fish Tank

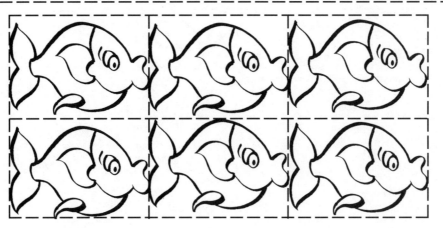

Parents: Explain to your child that he/she will use the fish from page 25 to measure these pictures.

How Many Fish Is It?

26

Measuring

Parents: Explain to your child what he/she is to do on this page. Have your child cut out the carrots at the bottom of the page to use as a measuring tool.

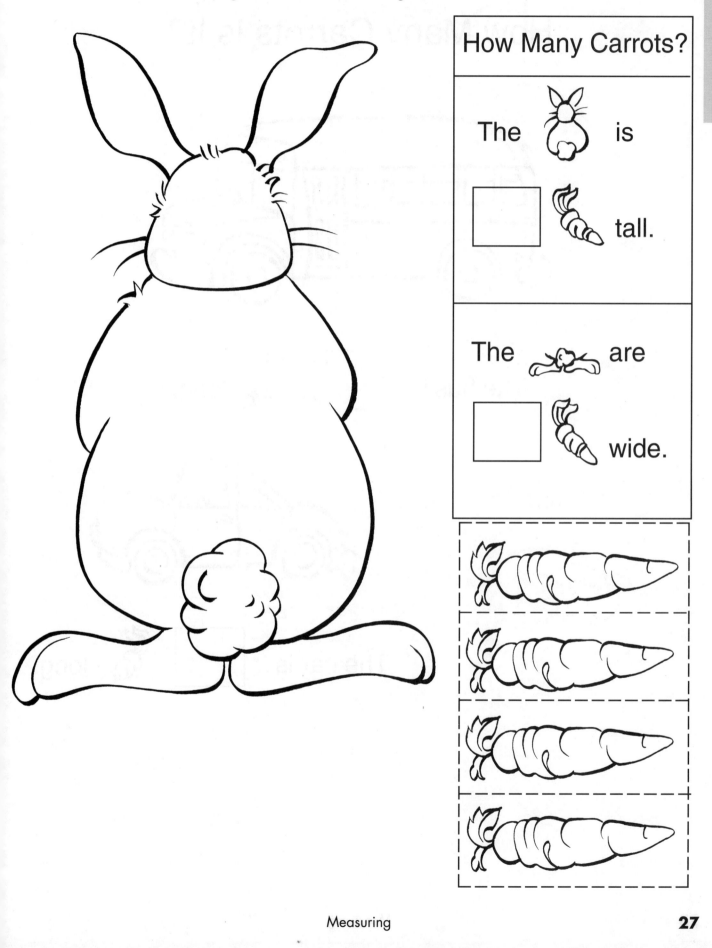

How Many Carrots?

The ![rabbit head] is

[ ] ![carrot] tall.

The ![carrot top] are

[ ] ![carrot] wide.

How Many Carrots Is It?

The bus is ☐  long.

The car is ☐ 🥕 long.

Parents: When you feel your child is ready to begin learning about standard measurement, use the ruler at the bottom of the page (or use a real ruler) and show him/her how to line it up at one edge of an object and to read the number at the other end of the object.

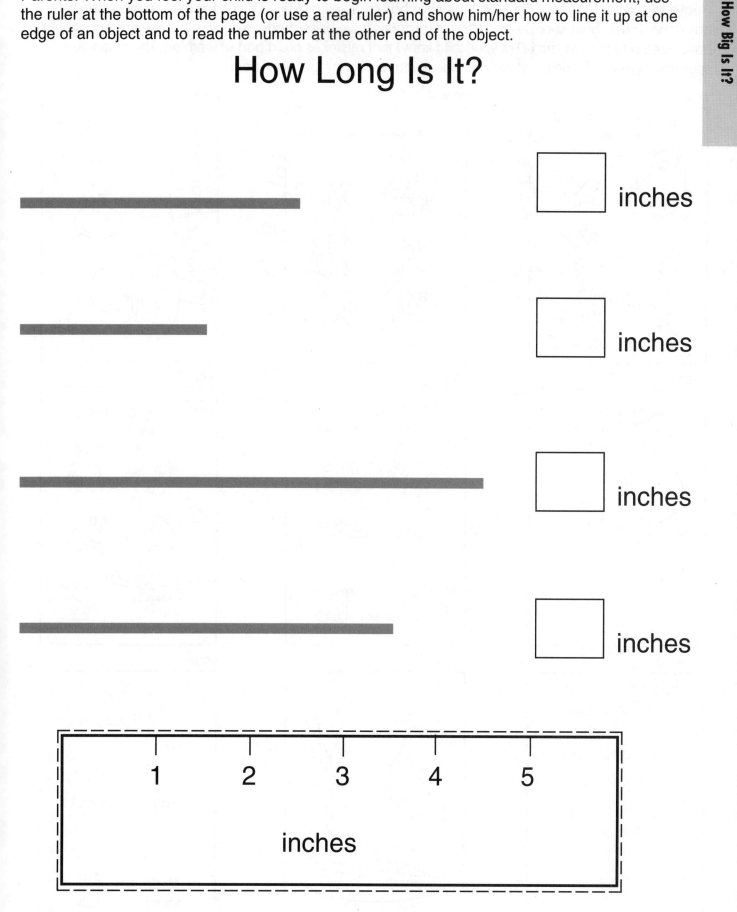

How Long Is It?

inches

inches

inches

inches

1   2   3   4   5

inches

Answer Key

Please take time to go over the work your child has completed. Ask your child to explain what he/she has done. Praise both success and effort. If mistakes have been made, explain what the answer should have been and how to find it. Let your child know that mistakes are a part of learning. The time you spend with your child helps let him/her know you feel learning is important.

page 3

page 4

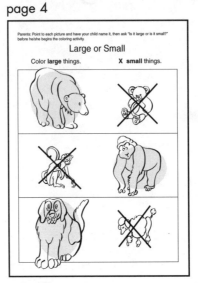

page 5

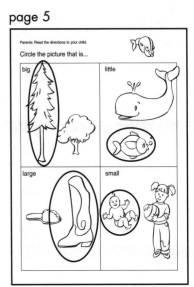

page 6

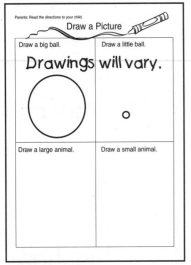

page 7

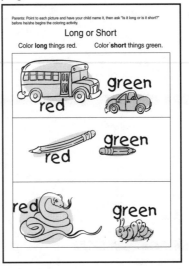

page 9

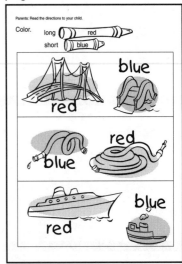

page 10

page 11

page 12

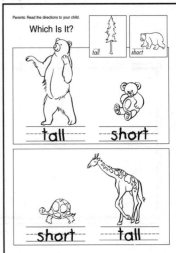

page 13

Parents: Read the directions to your child.

What Size Is It?

big   little

big   little

little   big

page 14

Parents: At this age your child needs to understand what happens when something is measured. He/she does not need to be using rulers and other measuring devices for a while. The activities on pages 13-28 will help develop this understanding. The activities use what is called non-standard measurement.

Measure the in s.

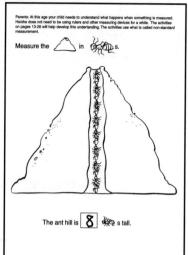

The ant hill is 8 s tall.

page 15

Measure the in s.

The wall is 4 s long.

page 16

Measure the in s.

The clothesline is 8 s long.

page 19

Answers will vary.

Parents: Explain to your child that he/she is going to measure things using the feet he/she made. The feet need to be laid heel-to-toe along whatever is ineing measured.

How Many Feet?

Measure your door in .

My door is

Measure your bed in .

My bed is

Measure you in .

I am

page 20

Answers will vary.

Parents: Explain to your child that he/she is going to use a big spoon to measure thing in the kitchen.

How Many Spoons?

page 21

Answers will vary.

Parents: Explain to your child that he/she is going to use measuring with small counters. You will need to provide coins for page 20, beans for page 21, and buttons for page 22. Show your child how to lay the counters along the picture being sure they are end to end.

Measuring with Coins

page 22

Measuring with Beans

Answers will vary.

Answers

page 23

Measure the Dog House

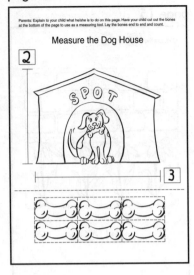

page 24

How many bones long it it?

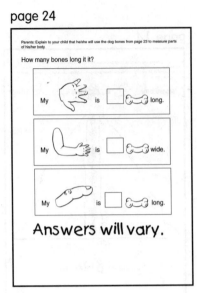

My ___ is [ ] ___ long.

My ___ is [ ] ___ wide.

My ___ is [ ] ___ long.

Answers will vary.

page 25

Measure the Fish Tank

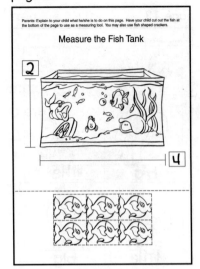

page 26

How Many Fish Is It?

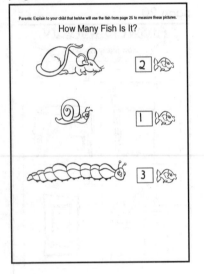

page 27

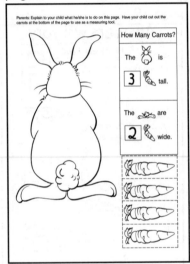

How Many Carrots?

The ___ is [3] ___ tall.

The ___ are [2] ___ wide.

page 28

How Many Carrots Is It?

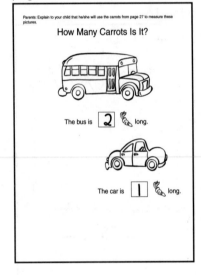

The bus is [2] ___ long.

The car is [1] ___ long.

page 29

How Long Is It?

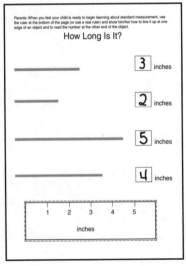

———— [3] inches

—— [2] inches

——— [5] inches

—— [4] inches

| 1 | 2 | 3 | 4 | 5 |

inches

Answers

Write the Numbers

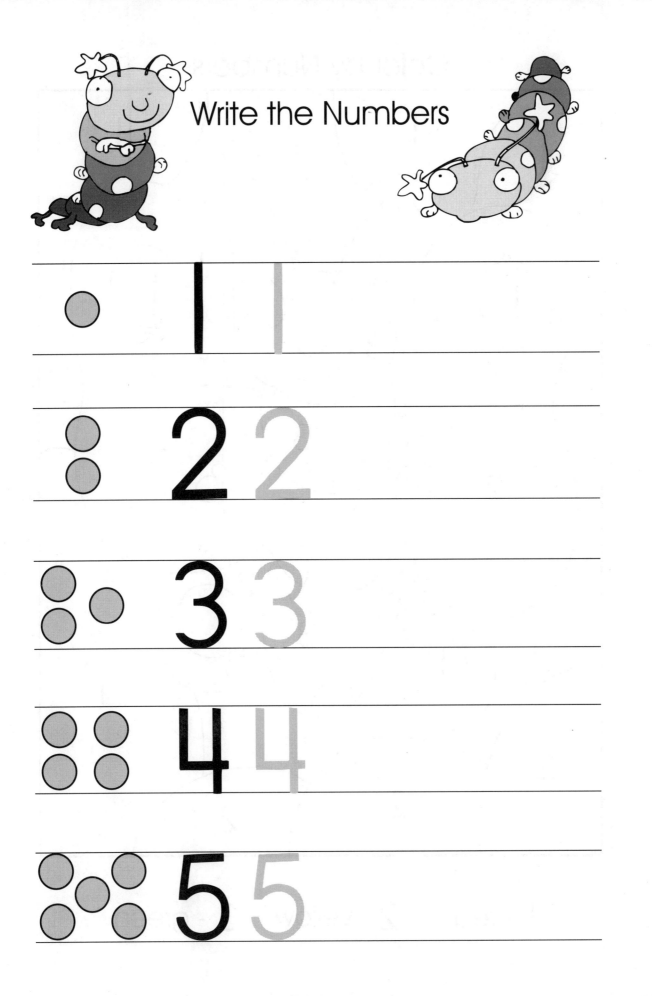

Color by Numbers

I - red   2 - yellow   3 - green

Count the bugs.
Circle the number.

0 1 ②3 4 5   0 1 2 3 4 5

0 1 2 3 4 5   0 1 2 3 4 5

0 1 2 3 4 5   0 1 2 3 4 5

Counting objects and matching with a number

How many do you see?

Counting objects and writing the number

Count the bugs.

How many? _____5_____

How many? _____

How many? _____

How many? _____

How many? _____

Counting objects and writing the number

Circle the set that has more.

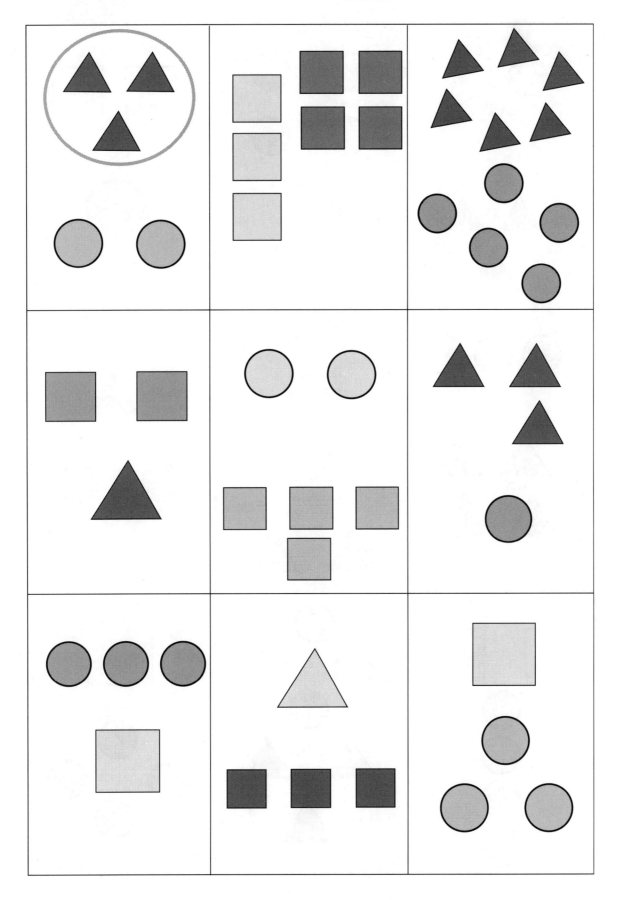

Put an X on the set that has less.

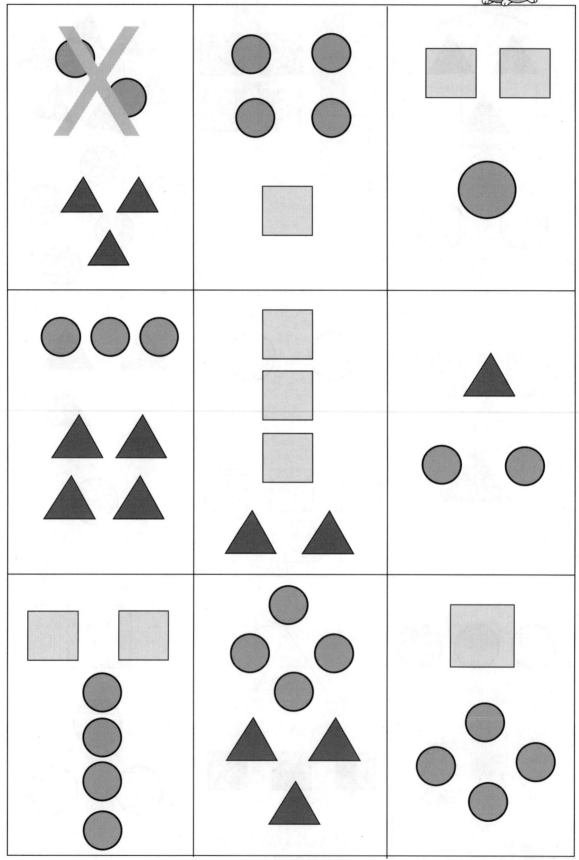

Understanding more and less

Color to find the ladybug.

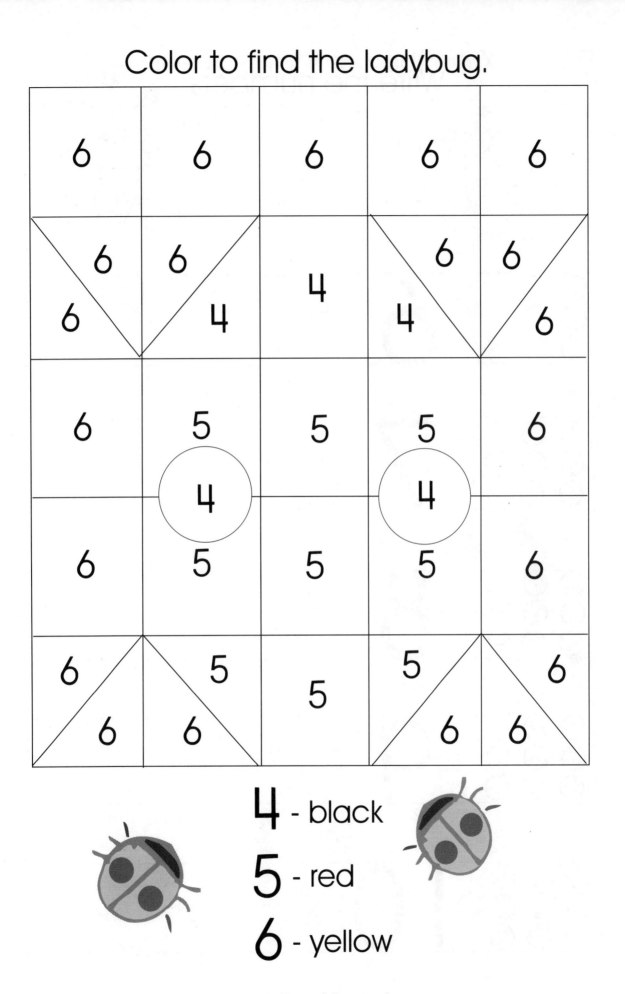

4 - black

5 - red

6 - yellow

Write the numbers.

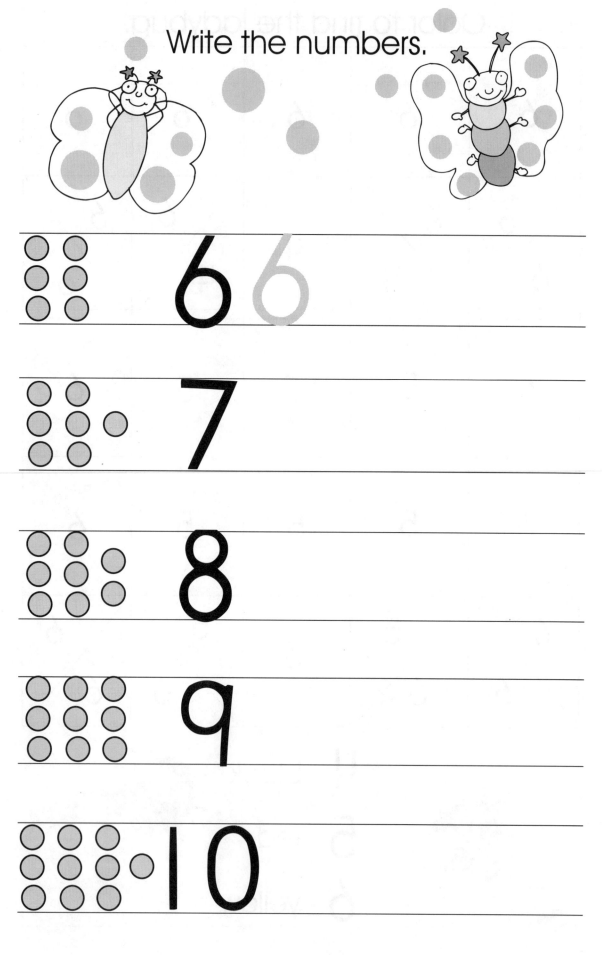

6 6

7

8

9

10

Writing numbers

Fill in the missing numbers.

1			4	
	7		9	

Find and circle the hidden numbers.

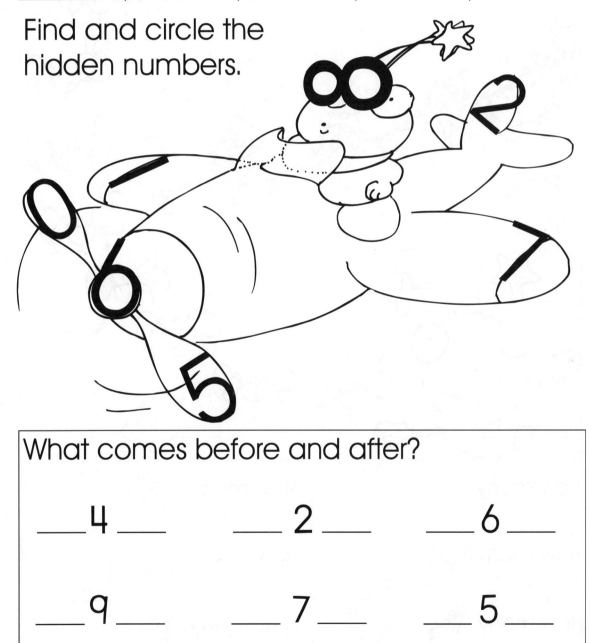

What comes before and after?

___ 4 ___   ___ 2 ___   ___ 6 ___

___ 9 ___   ___ 7 ___   ___ 5 ___

Count how many.
Put the number in the box.

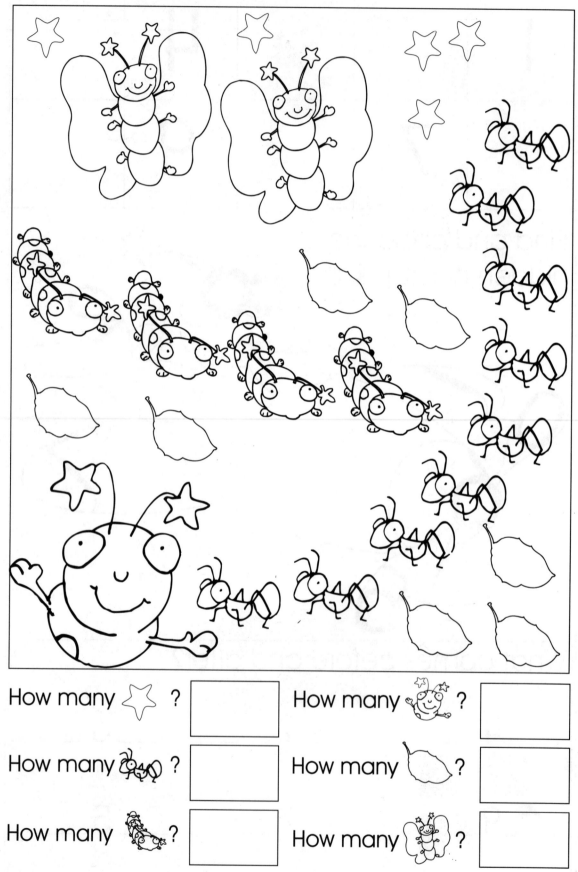

How many ☆ ? ☐ How many 🦋 ? ☐

How many 🐜 ? ☐ How many 🍃 ? ☐

How many 🐛 ? ☐ How many 🦋 ? ☐

Counting objects and writing the number

Circle the group that has more.

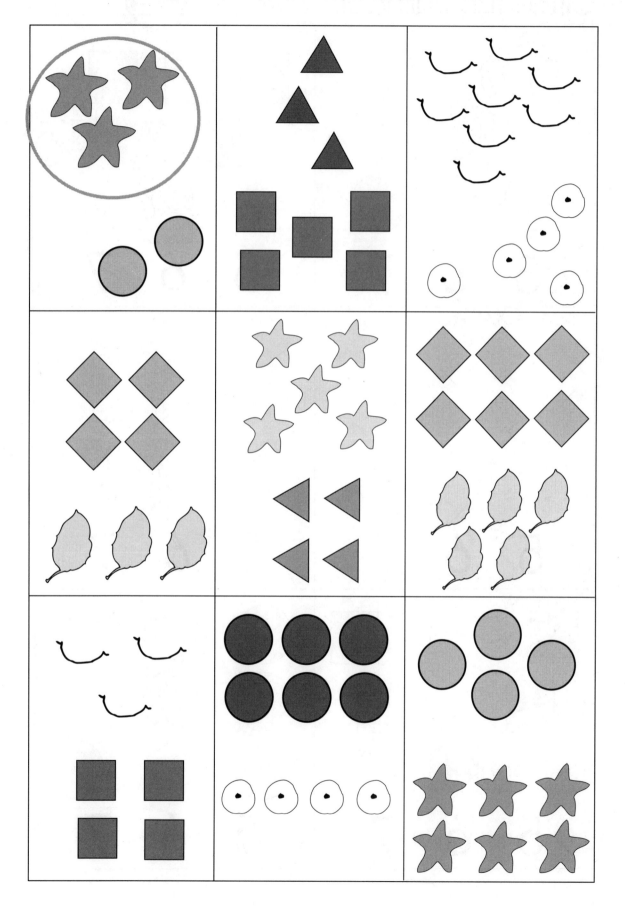

Count the set.
Circle the number

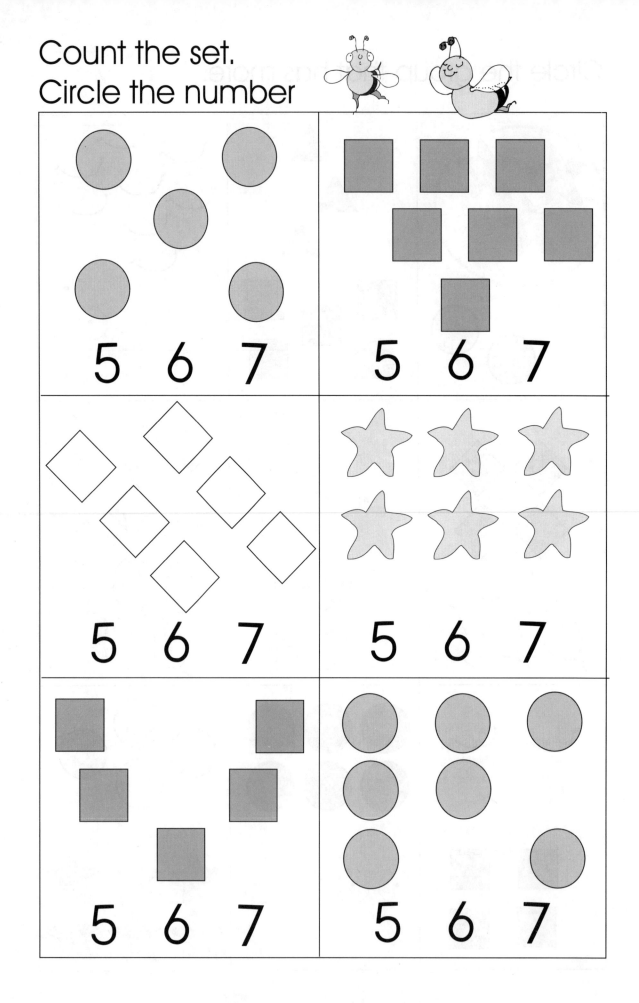

Counting objects and matching with a number

Start at the star.

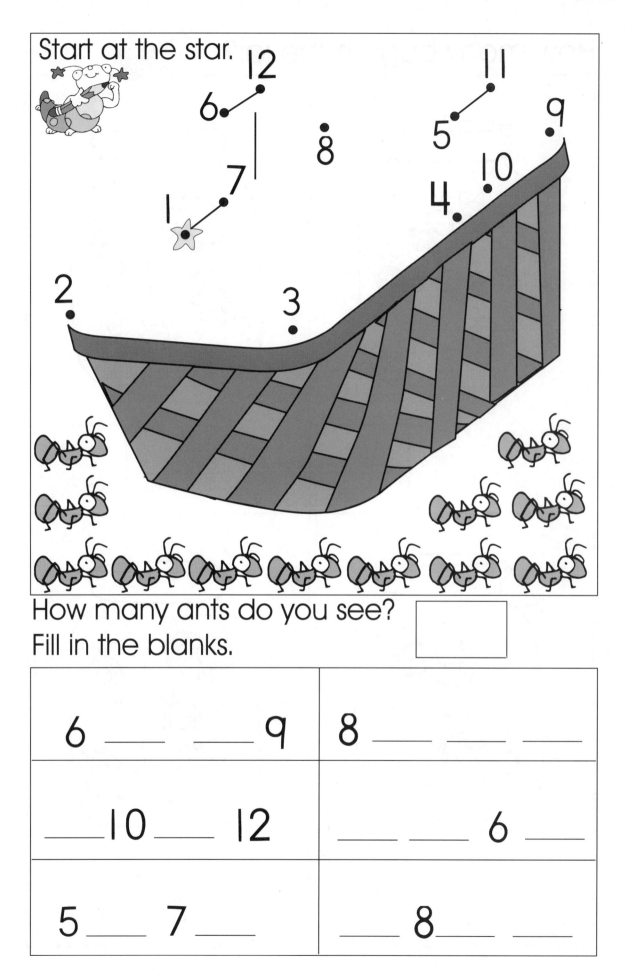

How many ants do you see? _____

Fill in the blanks.

6 ___ ___ 9	8 ___ ___ ___
___ 10 ___ 12	___ ___ 6 ___
5 ___ 7 ___	___ 8 ___ ___

How many bugs in the jar?

Counting objects and writing the number

Connect the dots from 1 to 10.

Put 4 spots on the ladybug

Understanding number order; understanding quantities represented by numbers

 # Make two matches.

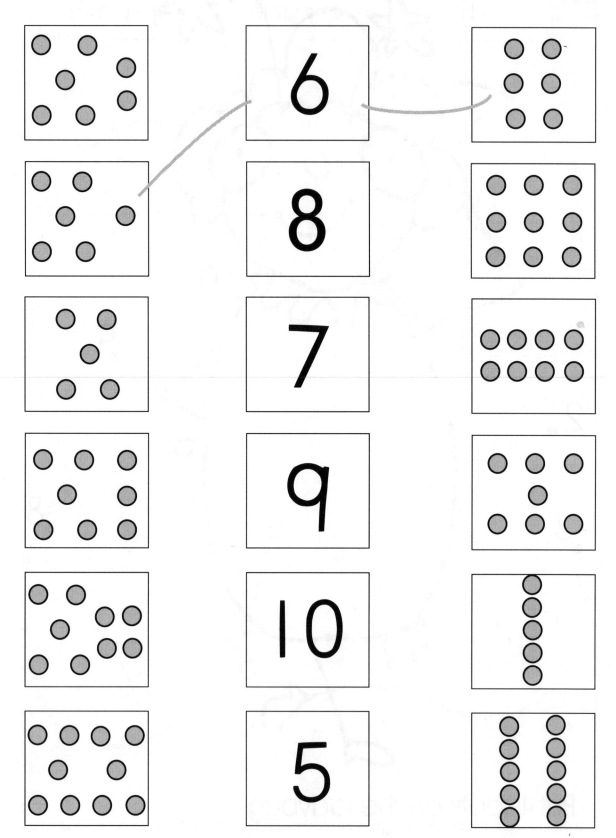

Counting objects and matching with a number

Find and color the numerals.

1 - red
2 - green
3 - blue

4 - orange
5 - yellow
6 - purple

7 - black
8 - white
9 - brown

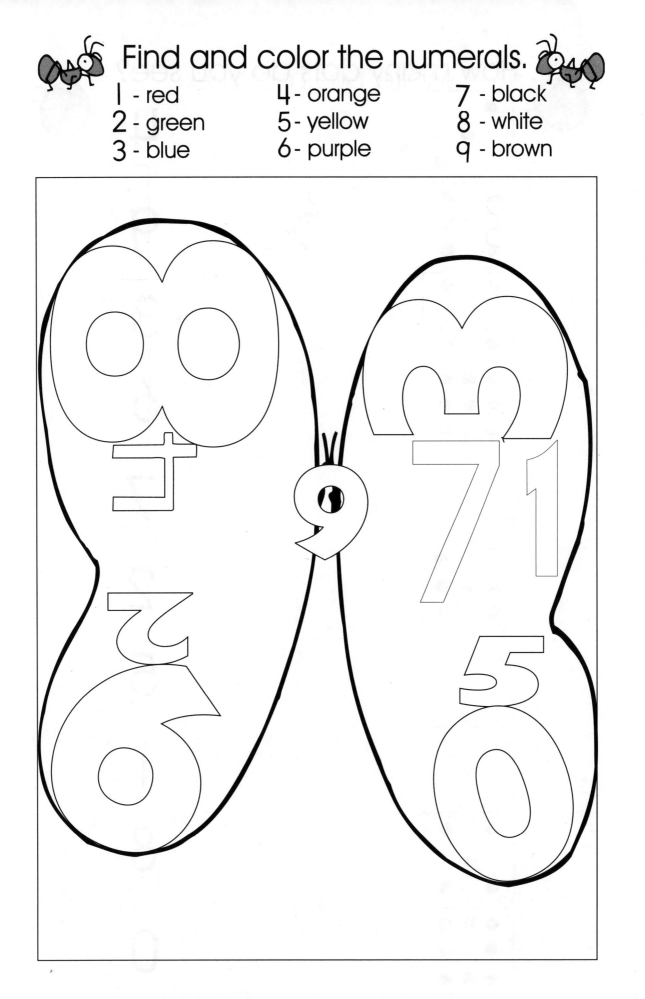

Recognizing numbers; following directions

How many dots do you see?

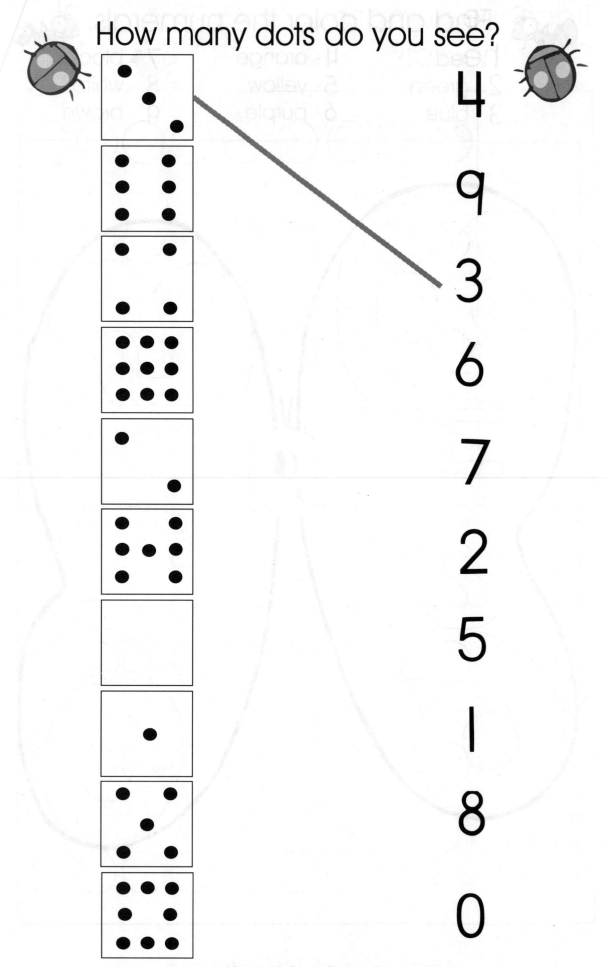

4

9

3

6

7

2

5

1

8

0

Counting objects and matching with a number

Trace the number.
Color the dots.

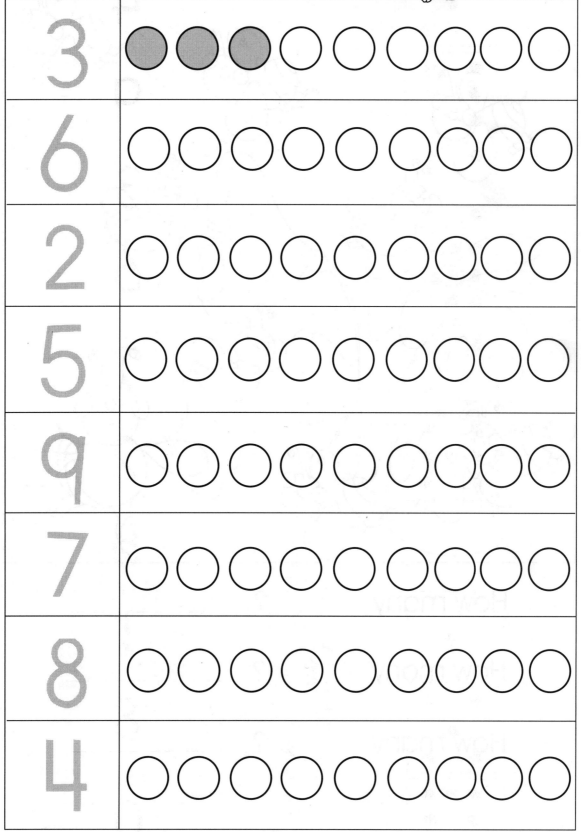

Understanding quantities represented by numbers

53

How many are there?

How many ![bee] ? _____

How many ![bee] ? _____

How many ![bee] ? _____

Counting objects and writing the number

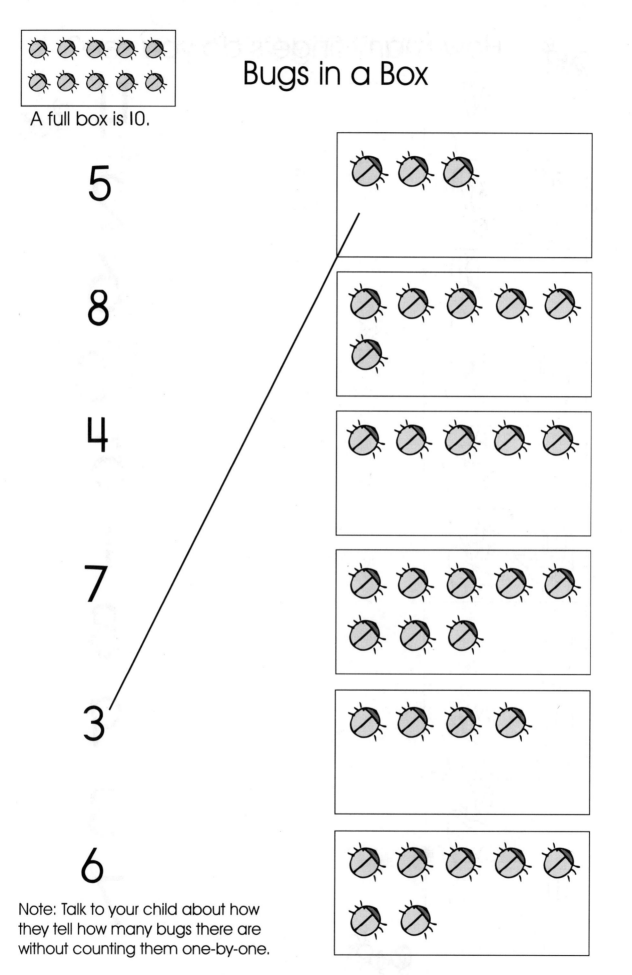

A full box is 10.

Bugs in a Box

5

8

4

7

3

6

Note: Talk to your child about how they tell how many bugs there are without counting them one-by-one.

Counting objects and matching with a number

How many fingers do you see?

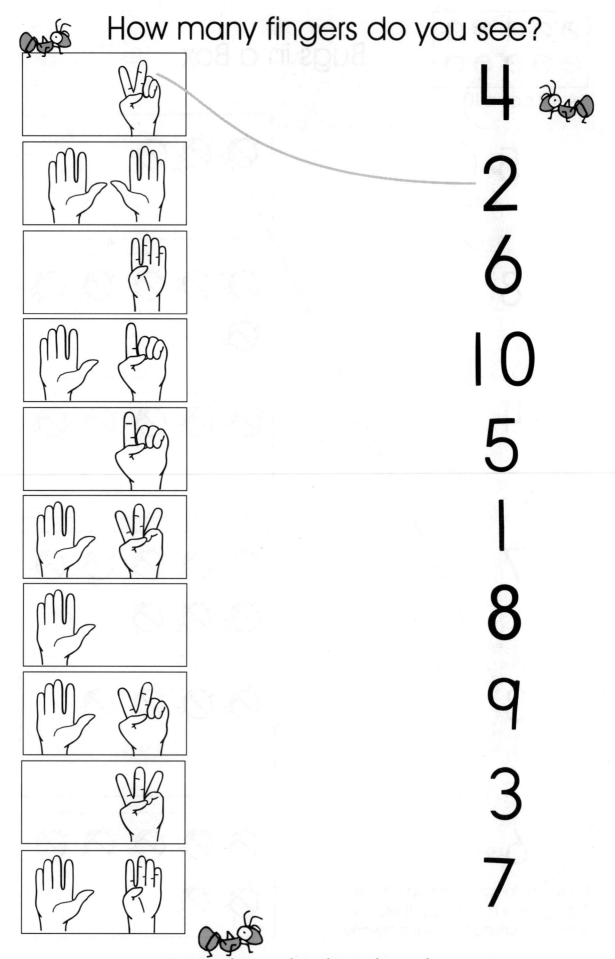

4

2

6

10

5

1

8

9

3

7

Counting objects and matching with a number

Circle the group that has more.

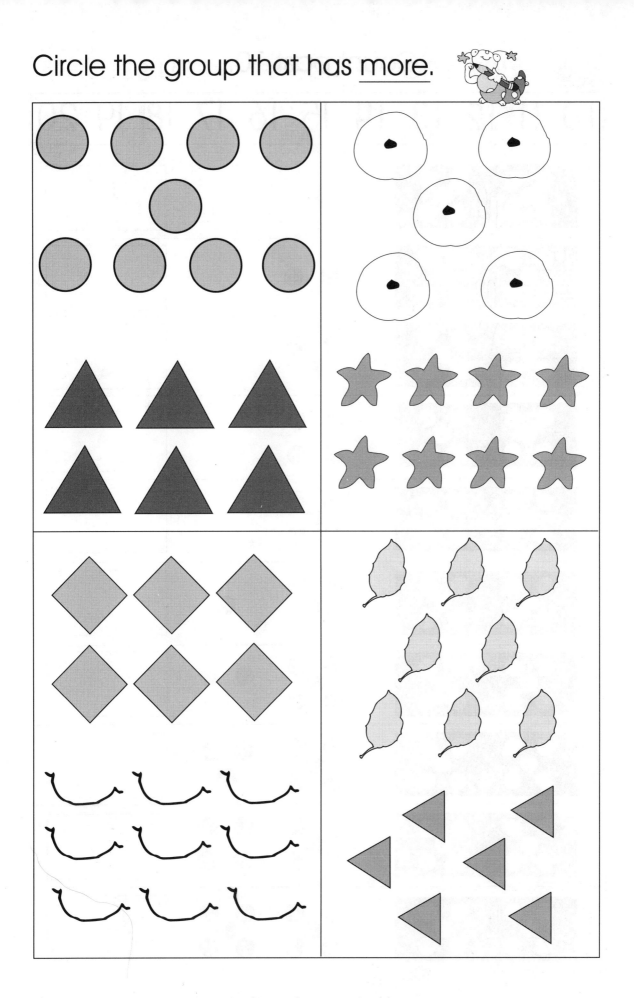

Count past 10.

| 10 | 11 | 12 | 13 | 14 | 15 | 16 | 17 | 18 | 19 | 20 |

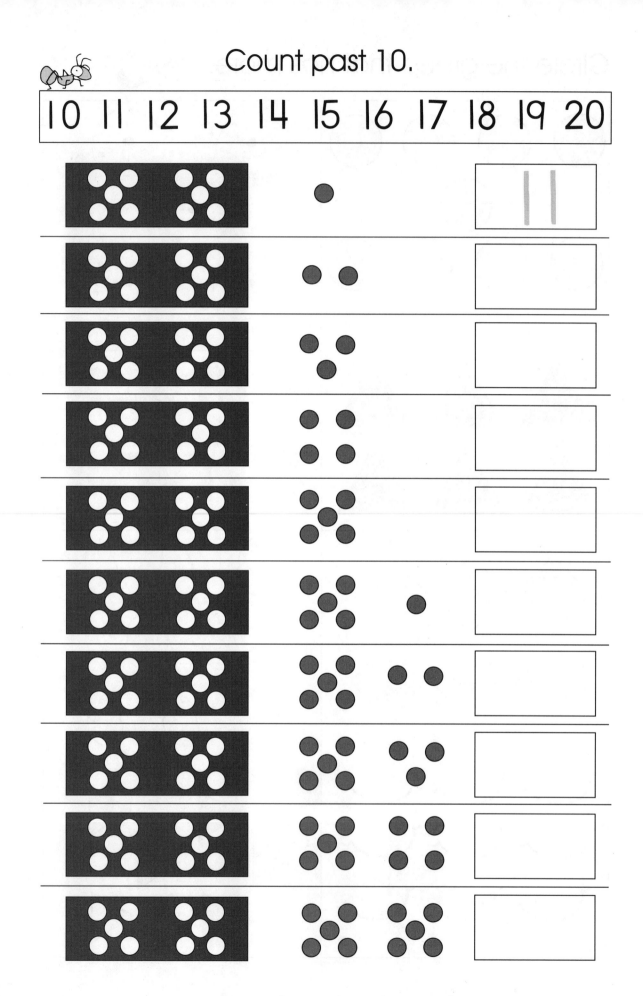

Counting objects and writing the number; more than 10

Ant Trail

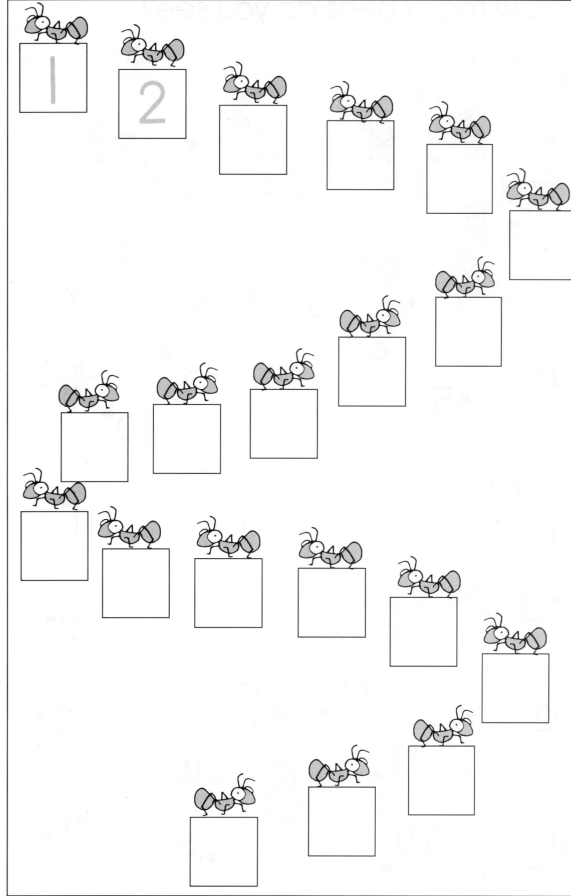

Understanding number order; writing numbers

59

How many bees do you see?

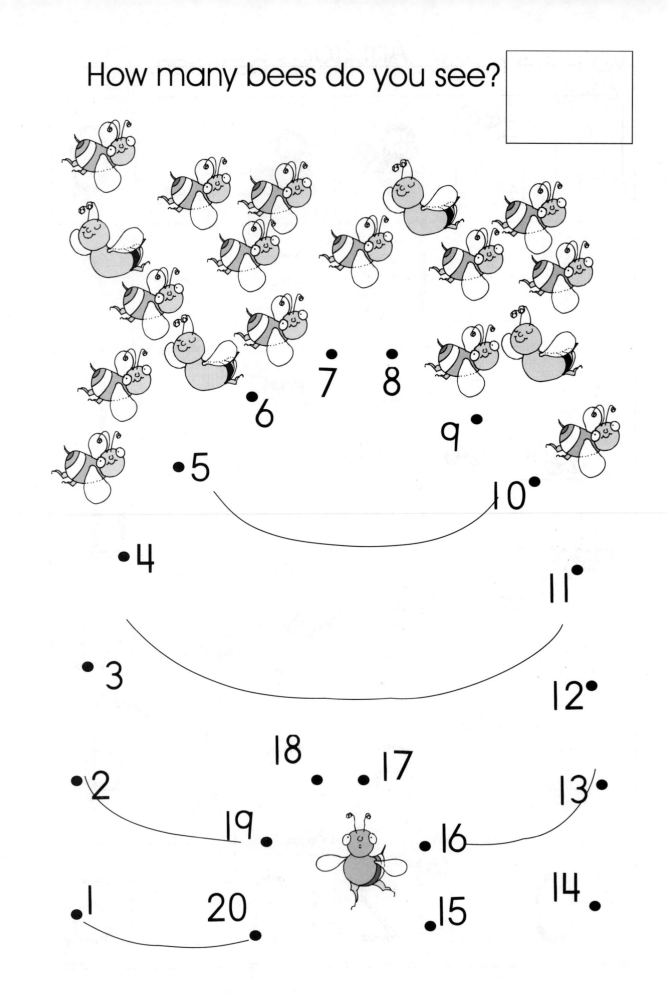

Counting objects; understanding number order

Write the number that goes between.

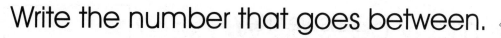

1 __2__ 3	8 ___ 10
11 ___ 13	5 ___ 7
4 ___ 6	9 ___ 11
14 ___ 16	2 ___ 4
6 ___ 8	12 ___ 14
3 ___ 5	7 ___ 9
10 ___ 12	13 ___ 15

Answer Key

Please take time to go over the work your child has completed. Ask your child to explain what he/she has done. Praise both success and effort. If mistakes have been made, explain what the answer should have been and how to find it. Let your child know that mistakes are a part of learning. The time you spend with your child helps let him/her know you feel learning is important.

page 34
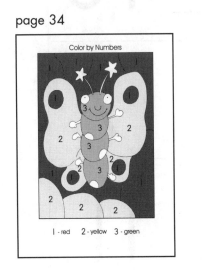

page 35
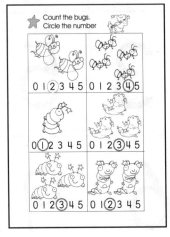

page 36
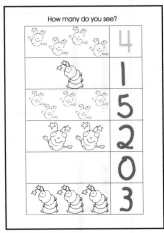

page 37

page 38

page 39
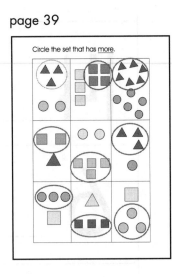

page 40
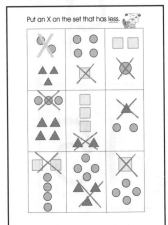

page 41
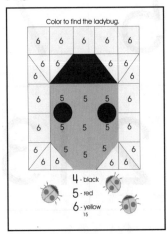

page 43
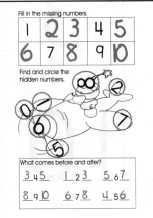

page 44

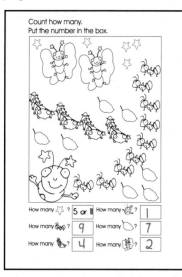

Count how many.
Put the number in the box.

How many ☆ ?	5 or 11	How many 🐜 ?	1
How many 🐛 ?	9	How many 🍃 ?	7
How many 🐛 ?	4	How many 🦋 ?	2

page 45

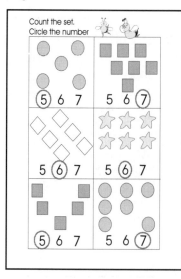

Circle the group that has more.

page 46

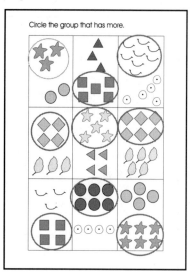

Count the set.
Circle the number

⑤ 6 7   5 6 ⑦

5 ⑥ 7   5 ⑥ 7

⑤ 6 7   5 6 ⑦

page 47

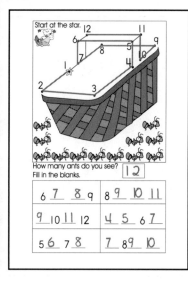

Start at the star.

How many ants do you see? 12
Fill in the blanks.

6 7 8 9	8 9 10 11
9 10 11 12	4 5 6 7
5 6 7 8	7 8 9 10

page 48

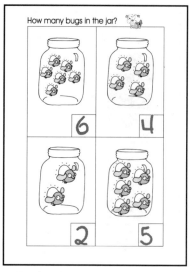

How many bugs in the jar?

6   4

2   5

page 49

Connect the dots from 1 to 10.

Put 4 spots on the ladybug

page 50

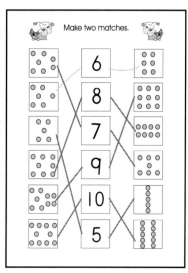

Make two matches.

6
8
7
9
10
5

page 52

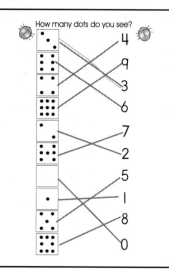

How many dots do you see?

4
9
3
6
7
2
5
1
8
0

page 53

Trace the number.
Color the dots.

3
6
2
5
9
7
8
4

page 54

How many are there?

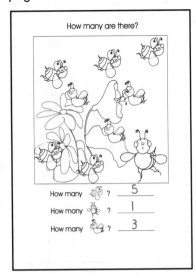

How many ?	5
How many ?	1
How many ?	3

page 55

A full box is 10.

Bugs in a Box

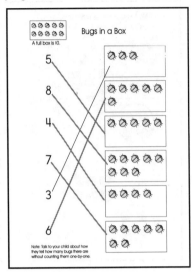

5
8
4
7
3
6

Note: Talk to your child about how they tell how many bugs there are without counting them one-by-one.

page 56

How many fingers do you see?

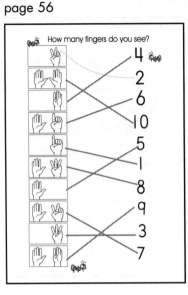

4
2
6
10
5
1
8
9
3
7

page 57

Circle the group that has more.

page 58

Count past 10.

| 10 | 11 | 12 | 13 | 14 | 15 | 16 | 17 | 18 | 19 | 20 |

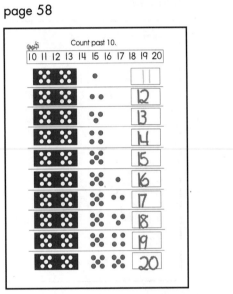

11
12
13
14
15
16
17
18
19
20

page 59

Ant Trail

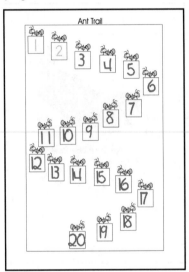

1 2 3 4 5 6 7 8 9 10 11 12 13 14 15 16 17 18 19 20

page 60

How many bees do you see? 19

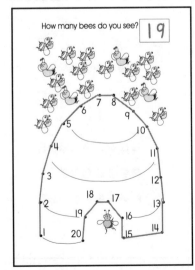

page 61

Write the number that goes between.

1	2	3	8	9	10
11	12	13	5	6	7
4	5	6	9	10	11
14	15	16	2	3	4
6	7	8	12	13	14
3	4	5	7	8	9
10	11	12	13	14	15

Answers

A Pair of Mittens

The 3 little kittens lost their mittens
And they began to cry.

Help the kittens find their mittens.
Color the mittens red.

I found _____ mittens. A pair is two mittens. I found _____ pairs of mittens.

Fun with Math

Make a Pair

Match.

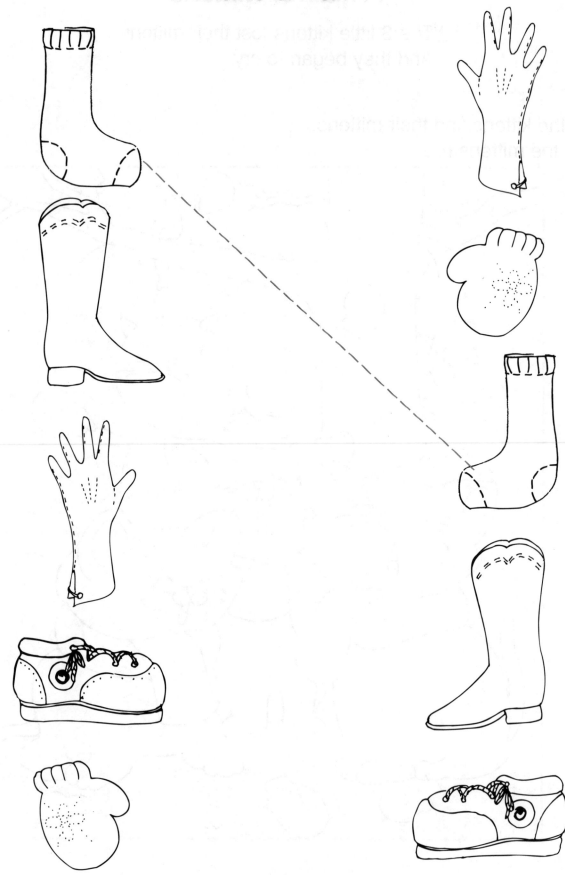

Matching pairs

Pairs

Give each kitten a pair of mittens.

Understanding one-to-one relationships

67

What Is the Number?

What is the number on your house?
Write it on this door.

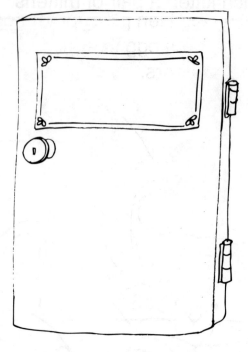

What is the number on your car?
Write it on this license plate.

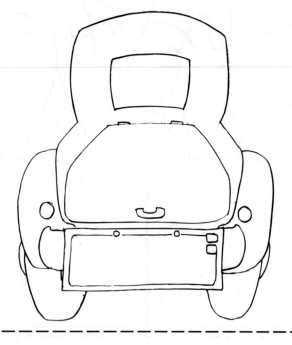

- -

Recognizing numbers; following directions

Little Red Hen

Help Little Red Hen pick up her eggs.
Draw a line from egg to egg.
Trace the numbers.

Fun with Math

12 Is a Dozen

Cut out the eggs on page 71.
Put the eggs in this egg carton.

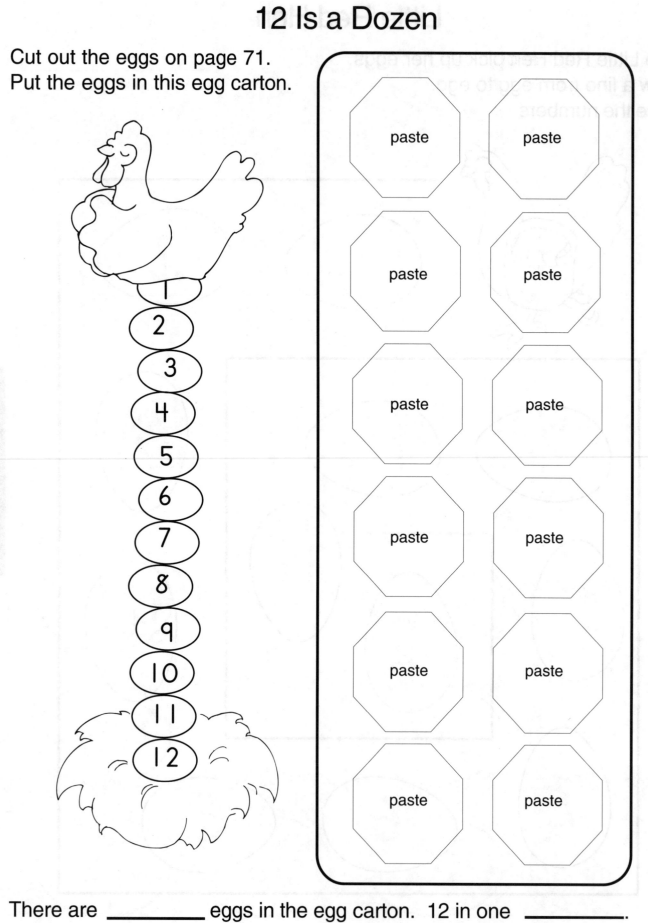

1
2
3
4
5
6
7
8
9
10
11
12

paste   paste

paste   paste

paste   paste

paste   paste

paste   paste

paste   paste

There are _____ eggs in the egg carton. 12 in one _____.

Following directions; using scissors; counting

Oval

Look at the shape of this egg. It is an oval.
Trace the oval.
Color it.

Cut out the eggs.
Paste them in the egg carton.

1 2 3 4

5 6 7 8

9 10 11 12

Recognizing shapes

Eggs in a Row

Look at the pattern.
Color the eggs.
What comes next?

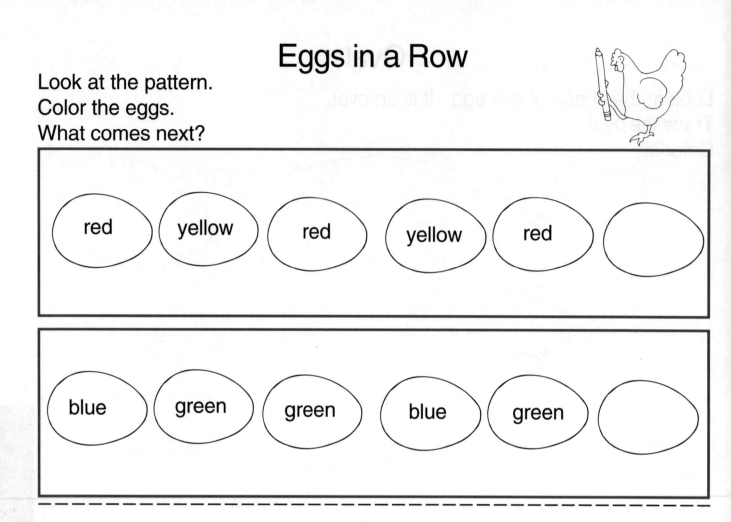

red | yellow | red | yellow | red |

blue | green | green | blue | green |

Completing patterns

Find the numbers hiding here.

Circle the numbers you found.

0   1   2   3   4   5   6   7   8   9   10

Who Is It?

Start at 1.
Connect the dots.

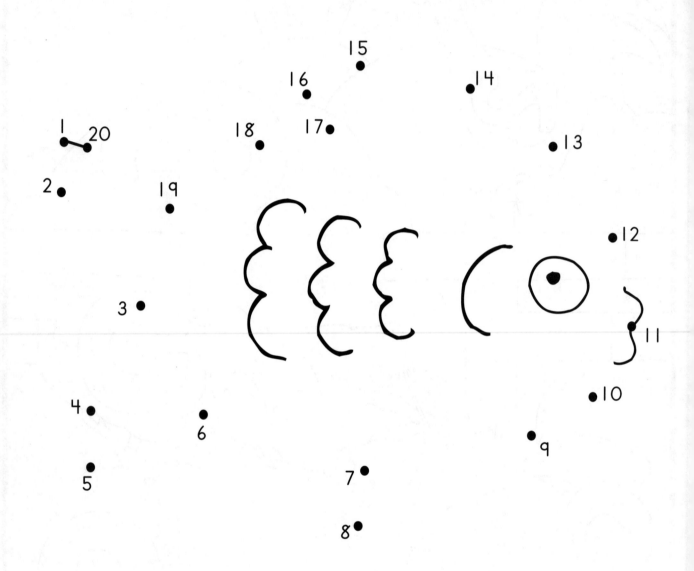

15
16
14
1 20
18 17
13
2
19
12
3
11
4 6
10
5
9
7
8

What did you find?

Fish

How many fish are in the bowl?

Trace.

Color.

Count.

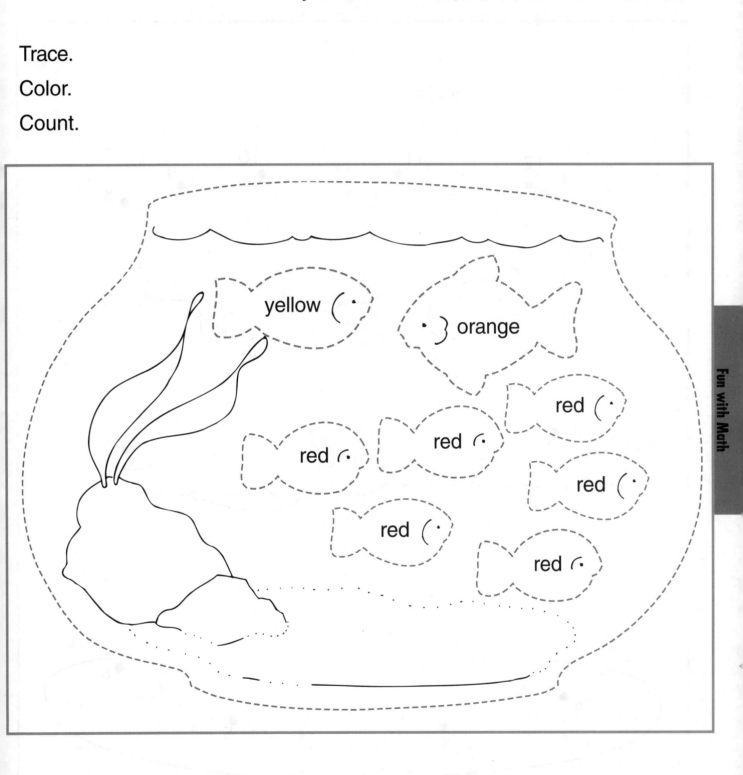

_____ fish are in the bowl.

What Is It?

Start at 1. Connect the dots.

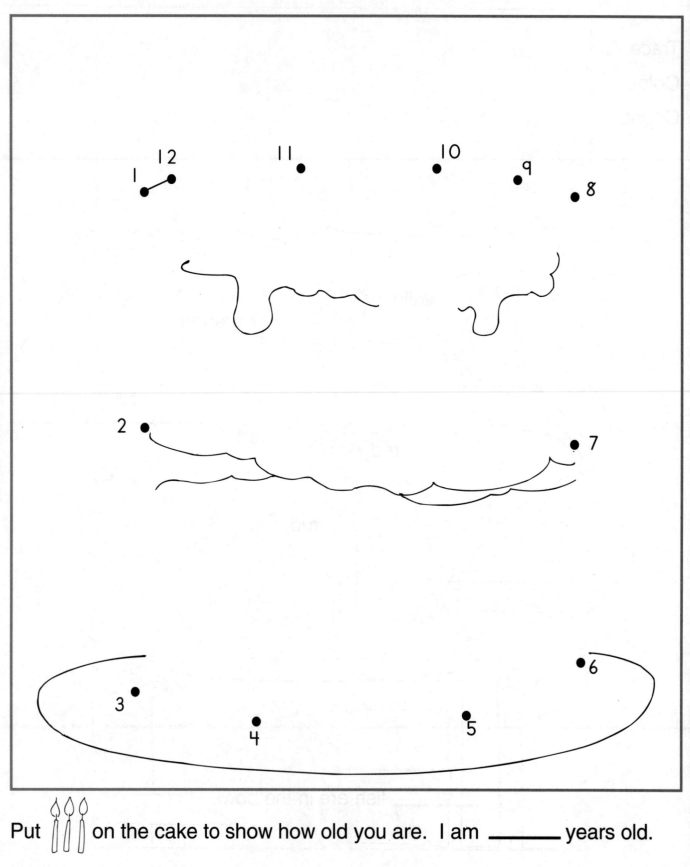

Put 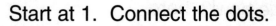 on the cake to show how old you are. I am _____ years old.

Understanding number order; following directions

The Presents

Put the puzzle together to see how many presents are here.

Birthdays in My Family

Find out when the people in your family were born.
Put their names and birthdays on this list.

_____'s Family Birthday List

Following directions; writing dates

Follow the Trail

Help the donkey find his tail. Fill in the missing numbers. Draw a line from the donkey to his tail.

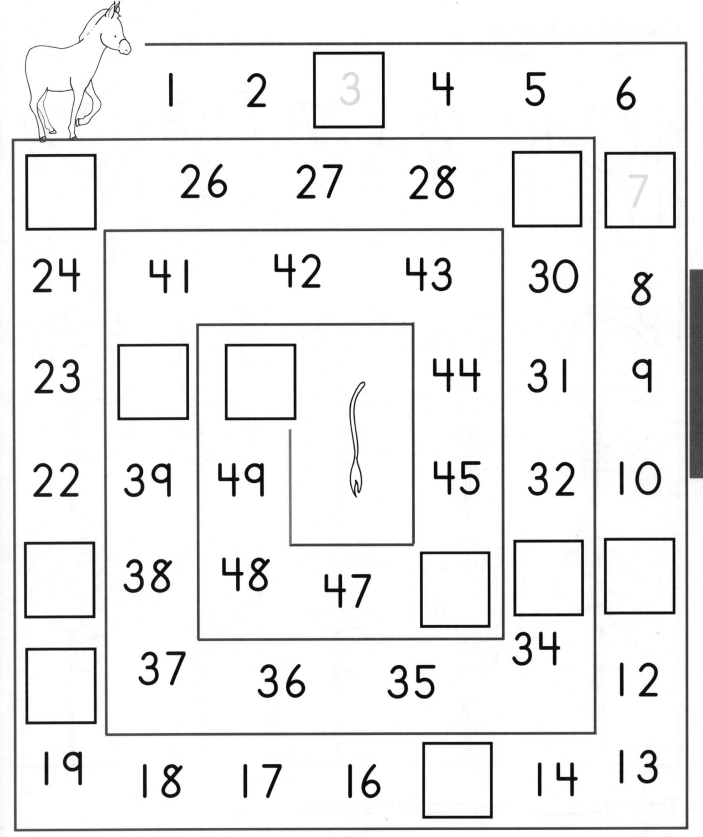

Mary's Flower Garden

Mary, Mary quite contrary
How does your garden grow?

Count Mary's flowers.

There are _____ flowers in Mary's garden.

Counting and writing the number

Color Fun

Find the shapes in Mary's garden.

Color red. ⃝

Color yellow. ⬡

Color orange. △

Fun with Math

Who Is Standing Here?

Start at 1.
Connect the dots.

Understanding number order

Feed the Elephants

Match the elephants to their peanut.

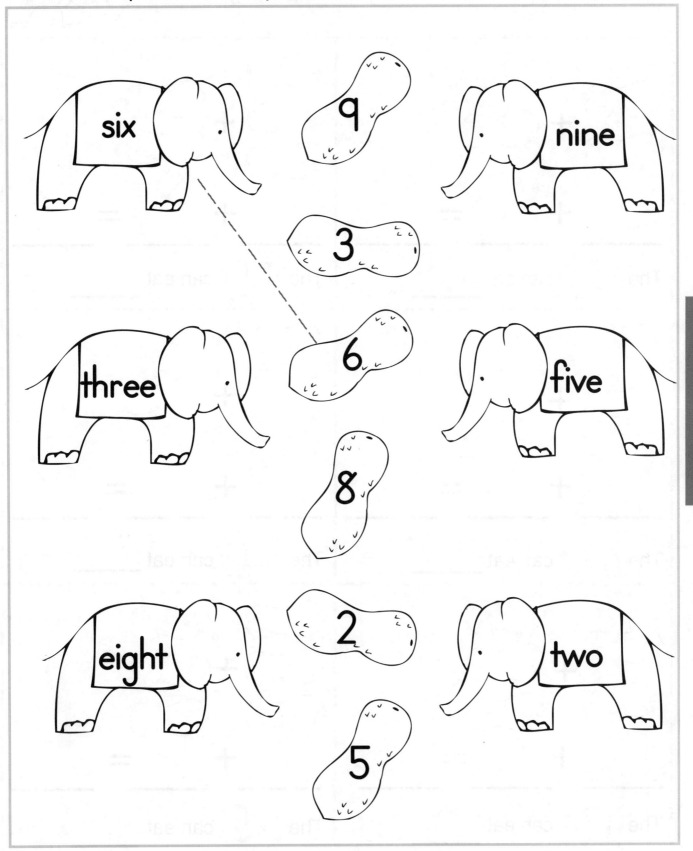

Feed the Elephant

Add the peanuts to see how many the elephant gets to eat.

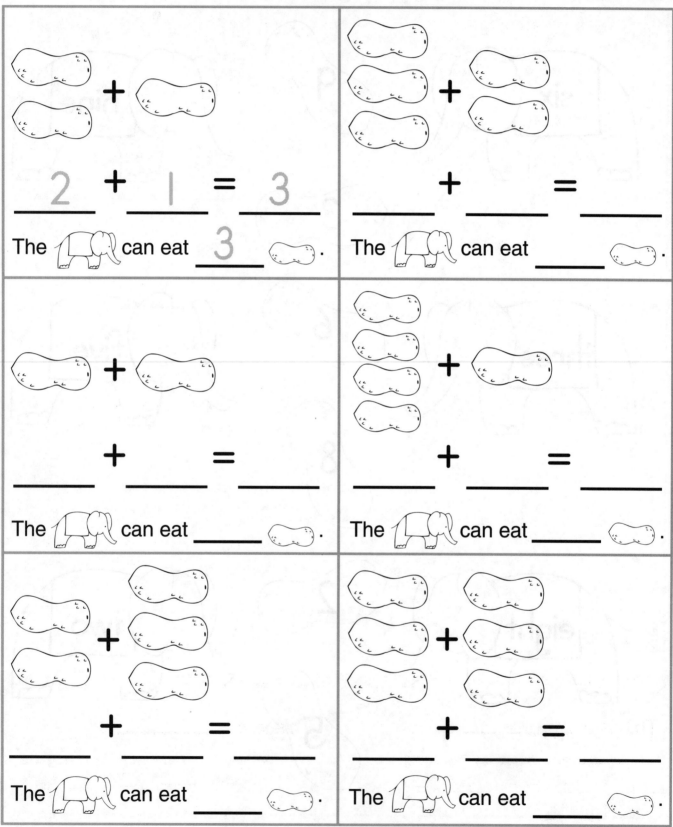

2 + 1 = 3

The can eat 3 .

_____ + _____ = _____

The can eat _____ .

_____ + _____ = _____

The can eat _____ .

_____ + _____ = _____

The can eat _____ .

_____ + _____ = _____

The can eat _____ .

_____ + _____ = _____

The can eat _____ .

Counting to add

Connect the dots to find the shapes.

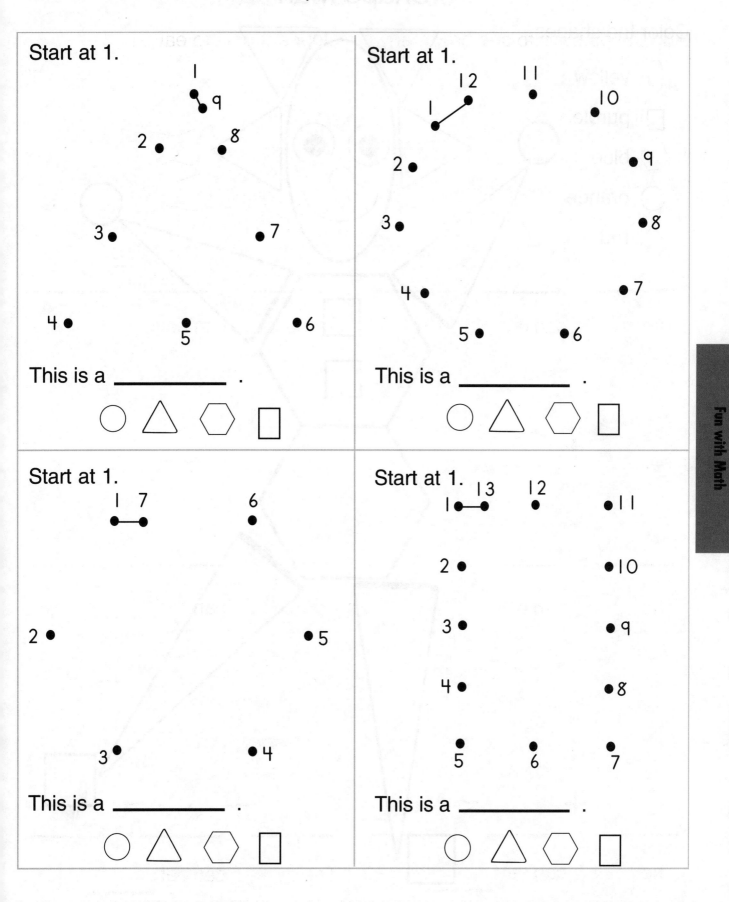

Start at 1.

1 9 8 2 3 7 4 5 6

This is a _____ .

Start at 1.

12 11 1 10 2 9 3 8 4 7 5 6

This is a _____ .

Start at 1.

1 7 6 2 5 3 4

This is a _____ .

Start at 1.

13 12 11 1 2 10 3 9 4 8 5 6 7

This is a _____ .

Shape Man

Color the shapes.

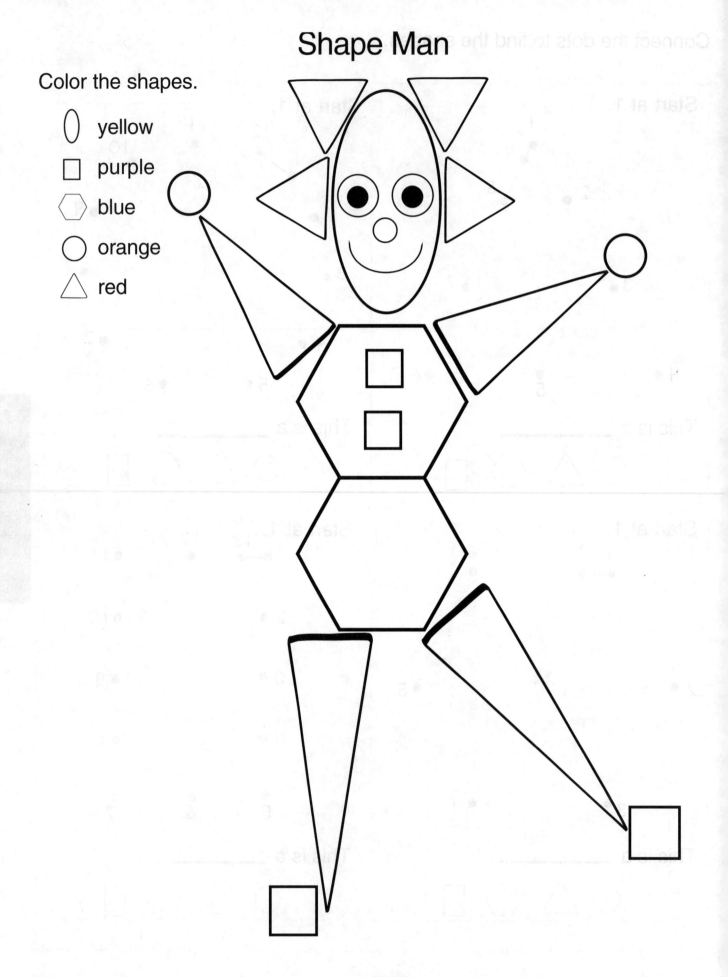

◯ yellow

▢ purple

⬡ blue

◯ orange

△ red

Recognizing shapes; following directions

The Clown

The clown has lost his hat.
Connect the dots to find it for him.

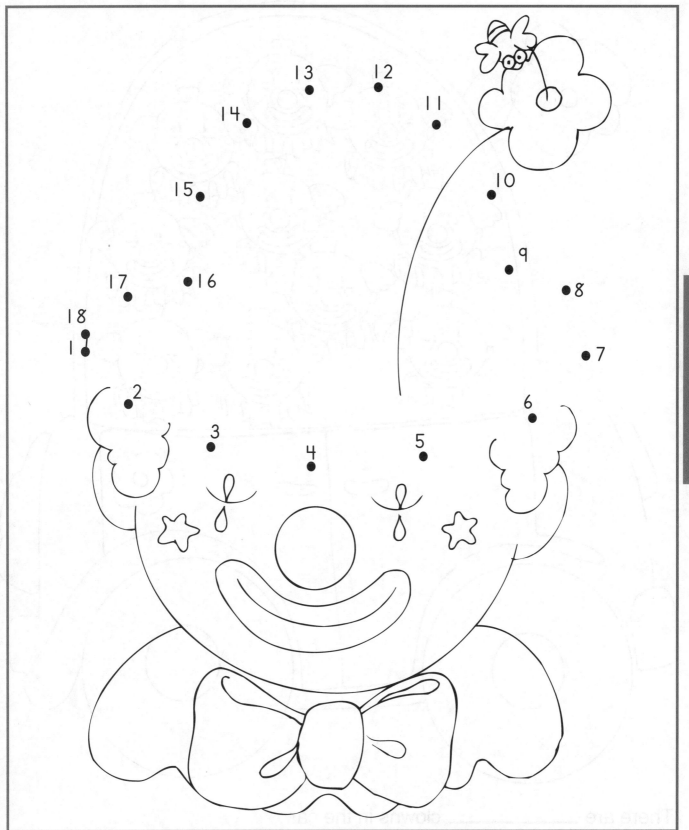

Clowning Around

How many clowns are inside this car?

There are _____ clowns in the car.

Counting objects and writing the number

Clowns in a Row

first   second   third   last

This clown is

_____

_ _ _ _ _ _ _ _ _

_____

in line.

This clown is

_____

_ _ _ _ _ _ _ _ _

_____

in line.

This clown is

_____

_ _ _ _ _ _ _ _ _

_____

in line.

This clown is

_____

_ _ _ _ _ _ _ _ _

_____

in line.

Fun with Math

Writing ordinal numbers

Hickory, Dickory, Dock

Hickory Dickory Dock.
A mouse ran up the clock.

Connect the dots to make the mouse's clock.

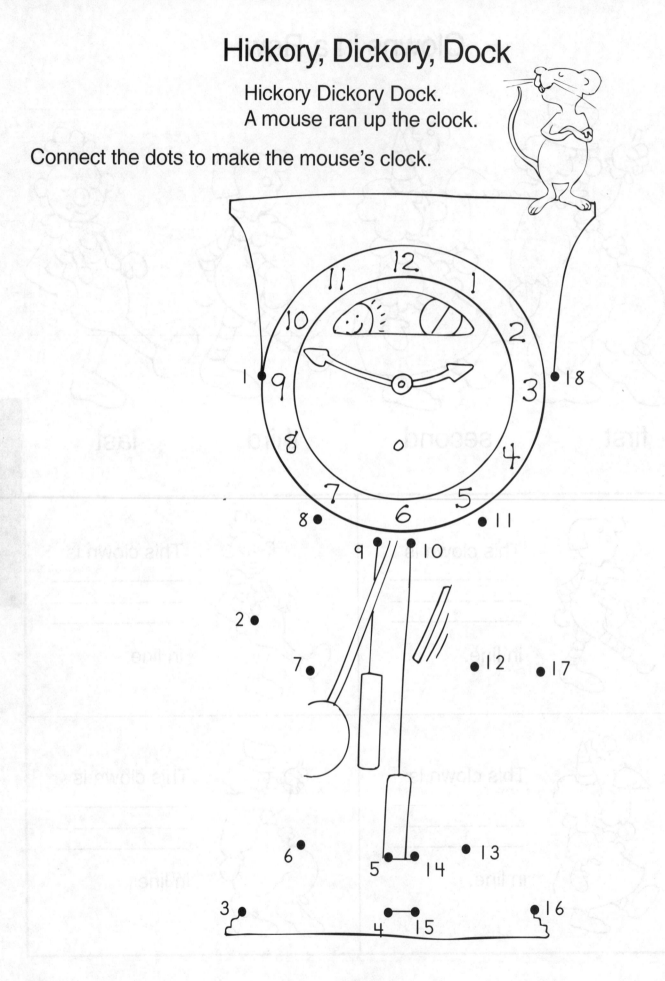

Understanding number order

What Time Is It?

What time is the little mouse showing you?
She is sitting on the hour hand.

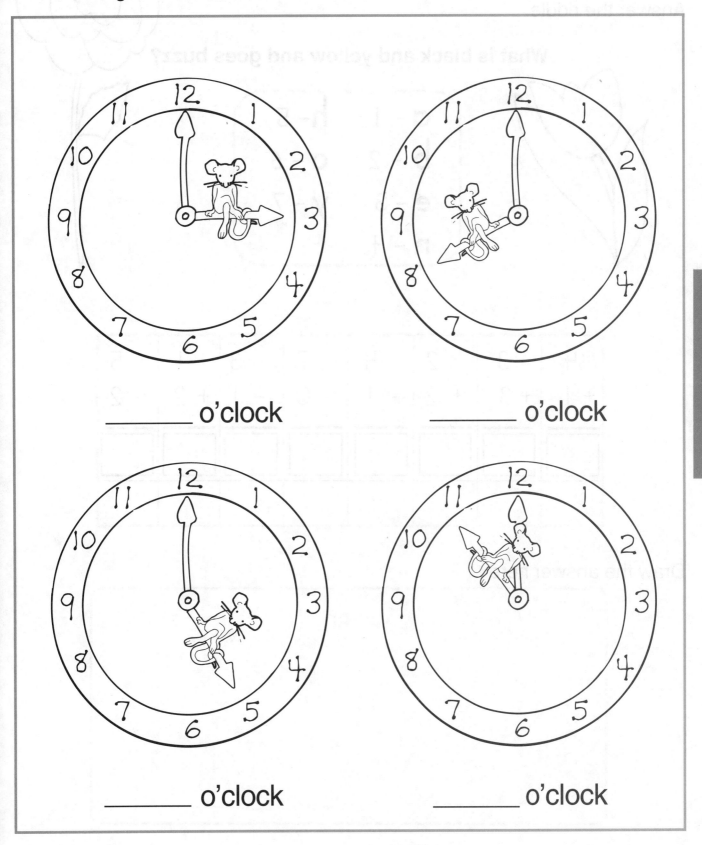

_____ o'clock

_____ o'clock

_____ o'clock

_____ o'clock

Fun with Math

Riddle

Work the problems.
Look at the code.
Answer the riddle.

What is black and yellow and goes buzz?

a – 1   h – 5
b – 2   o – 6
e – 3   y – 7
n – 4

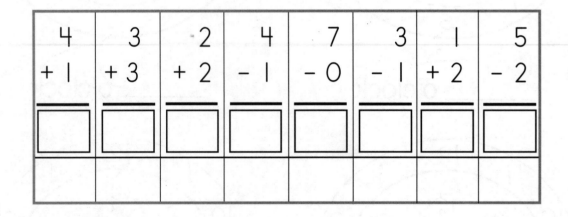

4 +1	3 +3	2 +2	4 -1	7 -0	3 -1	1 +2	5 -2
☐	☐	☐	☐	☐	☐	☐	☐

Draw the answer here.

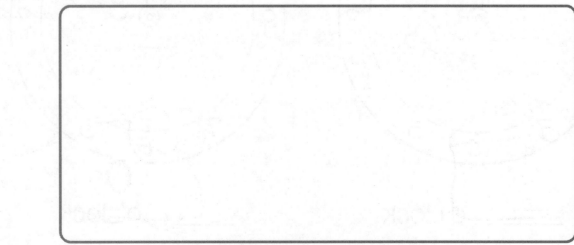

Following directions; adding and subtracting

Feed the Hungry Mouse

Match the 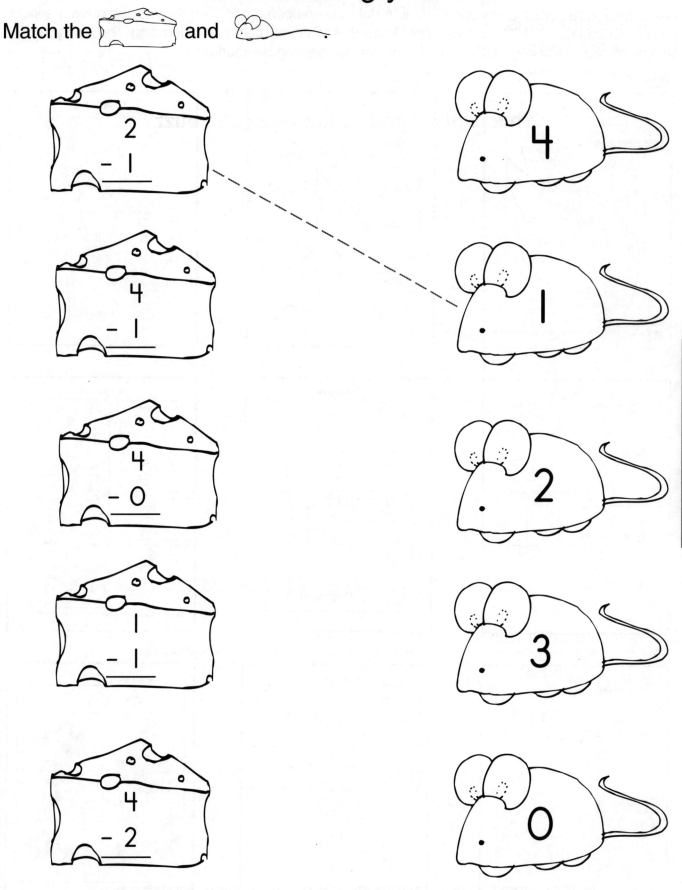 and

Fun with Math

Answer Key

Please take time to go over the work your child has completed. Ask your child to explain what he/she has done. Praise both success and effort. If mistakes have been made, explain what the answer should have been and how to find it. Let your child know that mistakes are a part of learning. The time you spend with your child helps let him/her know you feel learning is important.

page 65

A Pair of Mittens

The 3 little kittens lost their mittens
And they began to cry.

Help the kittens find their mittens.
Color the mittens red.

I found __6__ mittens. A pair is two mittens. I found __3__ pairs of mittens.

page 66

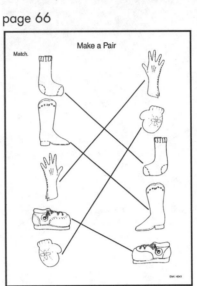

Make a Pair

Match.

page 67

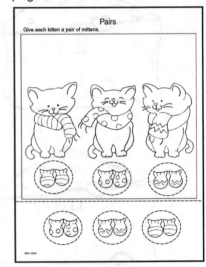

Pairs

Give each kitten a pair of mittens.

page 68

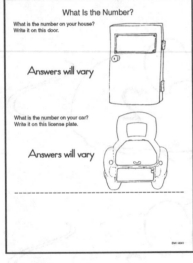

What Is the Number?

What is the number on your house?
Write it on this door.

Answers will vary

What is the number on your car?
Write it on this license plate.

Answers will vary

page 69

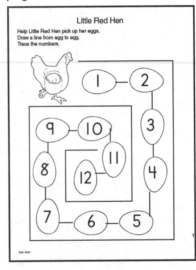

Little Red Hen

Help Little Red Hen pick up her eggs.
Draw a line from egg to egg.
Trace the numbers.

page 70

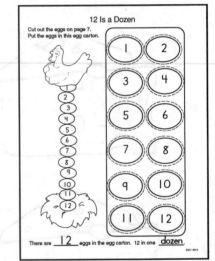

12 Is a Dozen

Cut out the eggs on page 7.
Put the eggs in this egg carton.

There are __12__ eggs in the egg carton. 12 in one __dozen__.

page 71

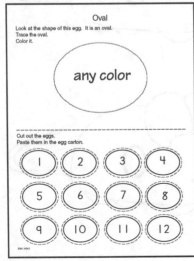

Oval

Look at the shape of this egg. It is an oval.
Trace the oval.
Color it.

any color

Cut out the eggs.
Paste them in the egg carton.

page 72

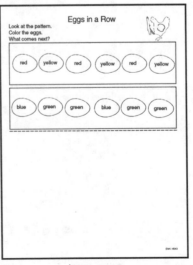

Eggs in a Row

Look at the pattern.
Color the eggs.
What comes next?

red   yellow   red   yellow   red   yellow

blue   green   green   blue   green   green

page 73

Find the numbers hiding here.

Circle the numbers you found.

0   1   ② ③ ④ ⑤ ⑥ 7   ⑧ 9   10

page 74

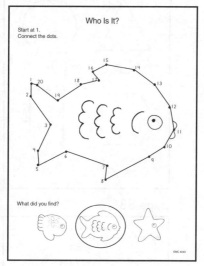

Who Is It?

Start at 1.
Connect the dots.

What did you find?

EMC 4043

page 75

Fish

How many fish are in the bowl?

Trace.
Color.
Count.

yellow

orange

red

red

red

red

red

__8__ fish are in the bowl.

EMC 4043

page 76

What Is It?

Start at 1. Connect the dots.

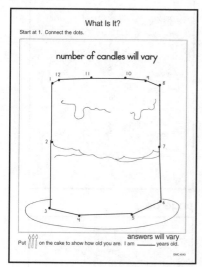

number of candles will vary

answers will vary

Put 🕯🕯🕯 on the cake to show how old you are. I am ____ years old.

EMC 4043

page 77

The Presents

Put the puzzle together to see how many presents are here.

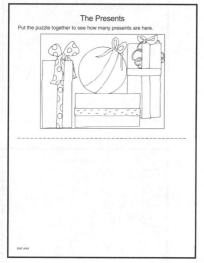

EMC 4043

page 78

Birthdays in My Family

Find out when the people in your family were born.
Put their names and birthdays on this list.

🕯🕯🕯 _____'s Family Birthday List 🕯🕯🕯

answers will vary

EMC 4043

page 79

Follow the Trail

Help the donkey find his tail. Fill in the missing numbers. Draw a line from the donkey to his tail.

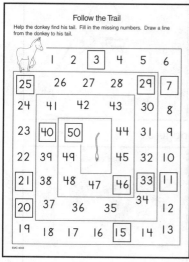

EMC 4043

page 80

Mary's Flower Garden

Mary, Mary quite contrary
How does your garden grow?

Count Mary's flowers.

There are __15__ flowers in Mary's garden.

EMC 4043

page 81

Color Fun

Find the shapes in Mary's garden.

Color red.
Color yellow.
Color orange.

orange

yellow

red

red

orange

orange

EMC 4043

page 82

Who Is Standing Here?

Start at 5.
Connect the dots.

EMC 4043

Answers

Fun with Math

95

Feed the Elephants

Match the elephants to their peanut.

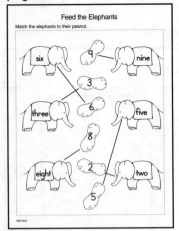

EMC 4043

Feed the Elephant

Add the peanuts to see how many the elephant gets to eat.

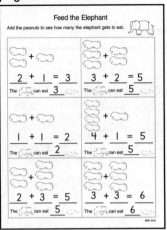

$2 + 1 = 3$ The elephant can eat 3

$3 + 2 = 5$ The elephant can eat 5

$1 + 1 = 2$ The elephant can eat 2

$4 + 1 = 5$ The elephant can eat 5

$2 + 3 = 5$ The elephant can eat 5

$3 + 3 = 6$ The elephant can eat 6

EMC 4043

Connect the dots to find the shapes.

Start at 1.
This is a (triangle).

Start at 1.
This is a (octagon).

Start at 1.
This is a (hexagon).

This is a (square).

EMC 4043

Shape Man

Color the shapes.

○ yellow
□ purple
○ blue
○ orange
△ red

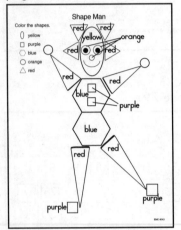

EMC 4043

The Clown

The clown has lost his hat.
Connect the dots to find it for him.

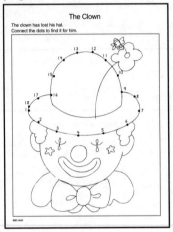

EMC 4043

Clowning Around

How many clowns are inside this car?

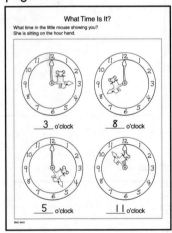

There are 10 clowns in the car.

EMC 4043

Clowns in a Row

first   second   third   last

This clown third is in line.

This clown last is in line.

This clown second is in line.

This clown first is in line.

EMC 4043

Hickory, Dickory, Dock

Hickory Dickory Dock.
A mouse ran up the clock.

Connect the dots to make the mouse's clock.

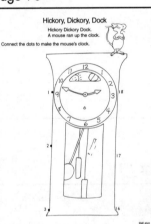

EMC 4043

What Time Is It?

What time in the little mouse showing you?
She is sitting on the hour hand.

3 o'clock

8 o'clock

5 o'clock

11 o'clock

EMC 4043

Riddle

Parents: Help your child read this riddle.

Work the problems.
Look at the code.
Answer the riddle.

What is black and yellow and goes buzz?

a - 1   h - 5
b - 2   o - 6
e - 3   y - 7
n - 4

4	3	2	4	7	3	1	5
+1	+3	+2	+0	-0	-1	+2	-2
5	6	4	4	7	2	3	3
h	o	n	e	y	b	e	e

Draw the answer here.

drawing of a bee

96

Feed the Hungry Mouse

Match the cheese and mouse.

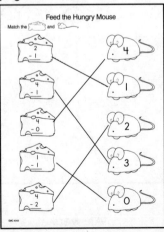

Answers

Parents:

Learning to tell time is an exciting achievement for children. They can tell when it's time for mother and/or father to get home from work, when their favorite television progams are on, when it's time to leave for a special outing, etc. It is a skill we take for granted since we learned how to do it so long ago. Some children find it easier to learn than others. Be patient and provide opportunities for your child to find out what time it is. The activities in this book will help you and your child reach this goal.

Go on a "Clock Search." (page 98)

Walk around the house with your child. Have him/her point out all the places that tell time. Point out places your child overlooks such as the clock on the microwave oven or the VCR. Have your child draw the time pieces he/she finds on page 98 of this book.

Make a paper plate clock (page 99)

You will need to provide your child with these items to use in making a clock face:

- 2 paper plates (or a cardboard circle and some scraps)
- a large paper fastener
- scissors
- glue
- sharp pencil

Steps to follow:

1. If your child can use scissors, have him/her cut out the clock face and the hands on page 99. If not, cut the pieces out yourself.

2. Help your child glue the clock face to one paper plate and the hands to the second paper plate. After the glue has dried, cut the hands out again (the paper plate will give them added strength).

3. Use the pencil to poke a hole in the clock and hands where marked with a small circle. You will need to do this for your child.

4. Place the hands on the clock face and attach them with the paper fastener. Move the hands around a few times to be sure they are moving freely.

Your child will need this clock several times while doing the activities in this book.

Parents: Read the directions for a clock search on page 97.

I'm Going on a Clock Search

Look.
Draw.

Recognizing clocks

My Own Clock

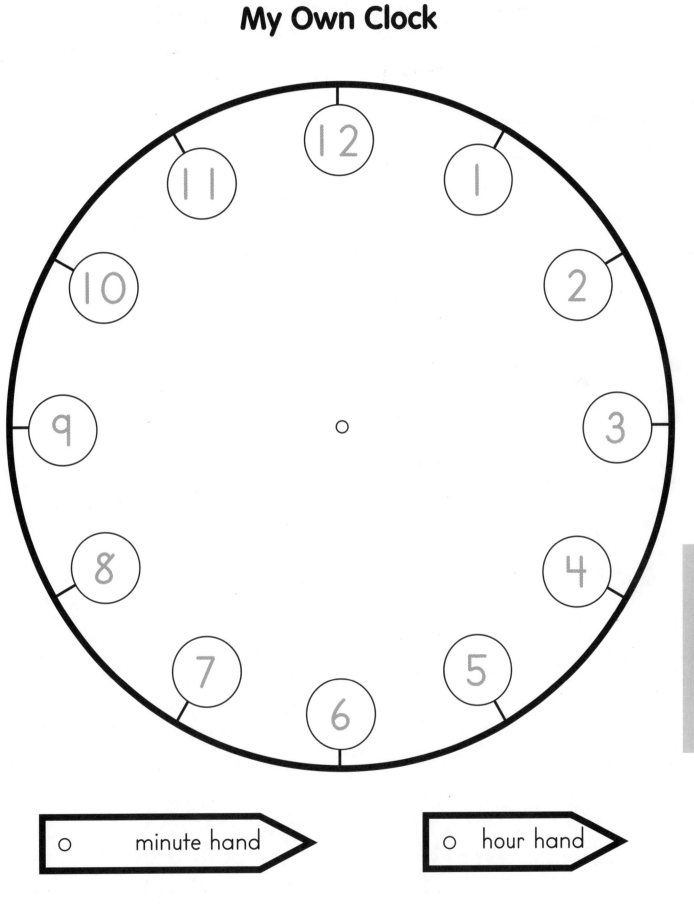

Parents: Point out to your child that the clock front is called the face and that the pieces that move around are called hands.

Color the Hands

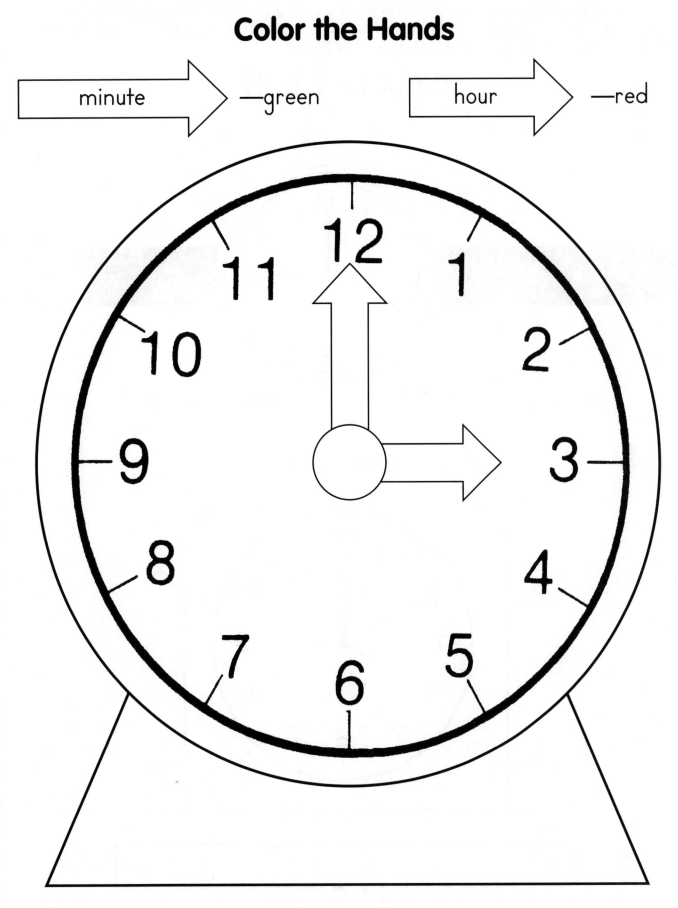

Parents: Explain to your child that when the big hand is on the 12, we look at the little hand to see what hour it is. Practice with the paper plate clock, having your child put the long hand on the 12 and the little hand pointing to each number in turn. Have him/her say "It is _3 o'clock_." and so on as the little hand is moved. Then look at the clocks on this page. Have your child tell you the hour.

What time is it?

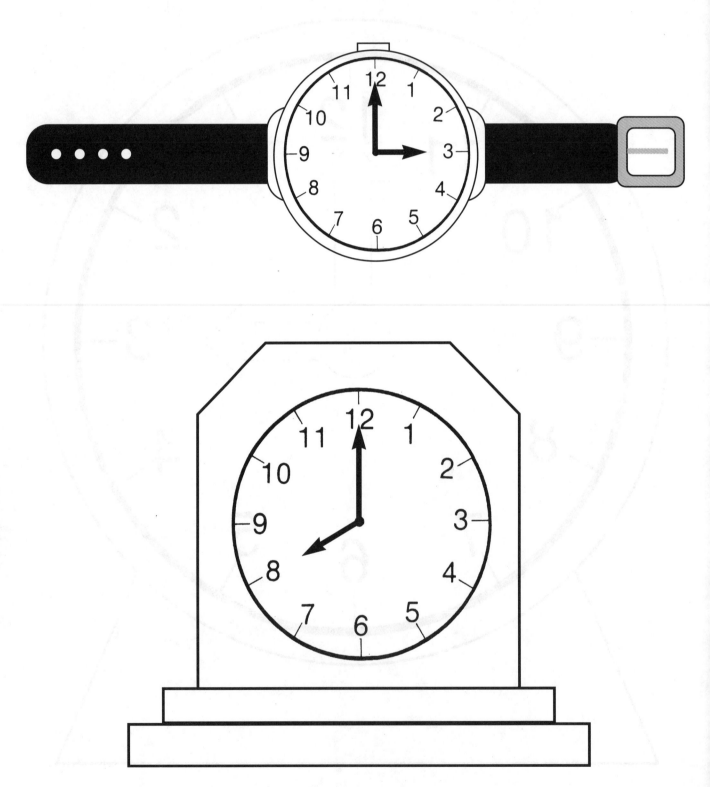

Telling time to the hour

What time is it?

Circle the time.

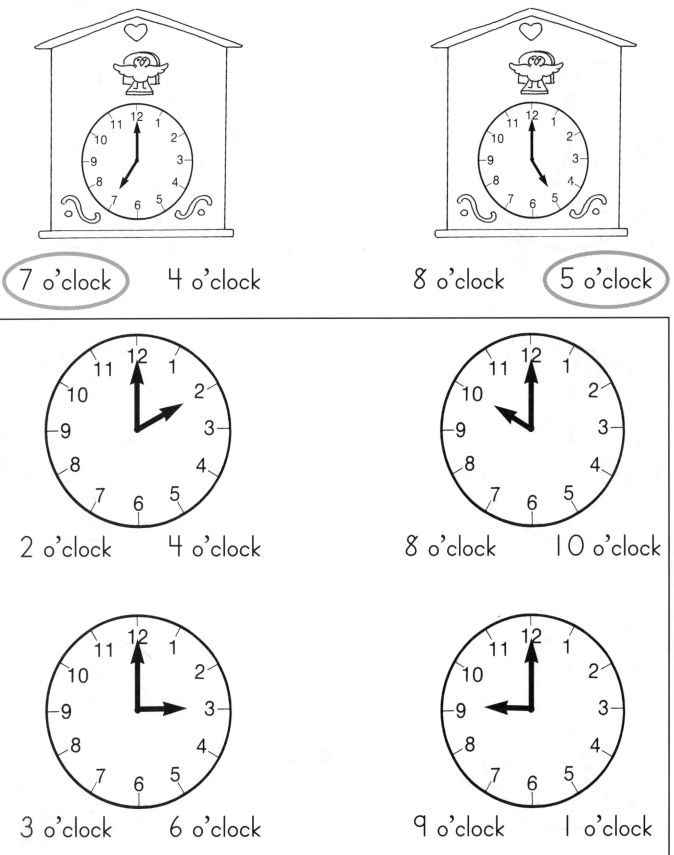

(7 o'clock)   4 o'clock   8 o'clock   (5 o'clock)

2 o'clock   4 o'clock   8 o'clock   10 o'clock

3 o'clock   6 o'clock   9 o'clock   1 o'clock

Telling time to the hour

What time is it?

Match the clock to the hour.

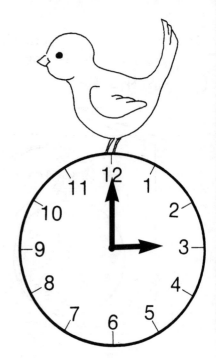

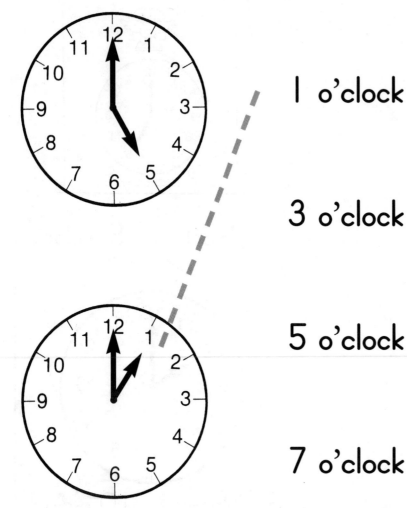

1 o'clock

3 o'clock

5 o'clock

7 o'clock

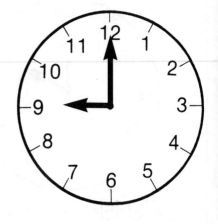

9 o'clock

11 o'clock

Parents: Explain to your child that time is written in a special way. Show the examples on this page, then have your child write the correct time.

What time is it?

3:00

9:00

:00

:00

:00

:00

Write the time.

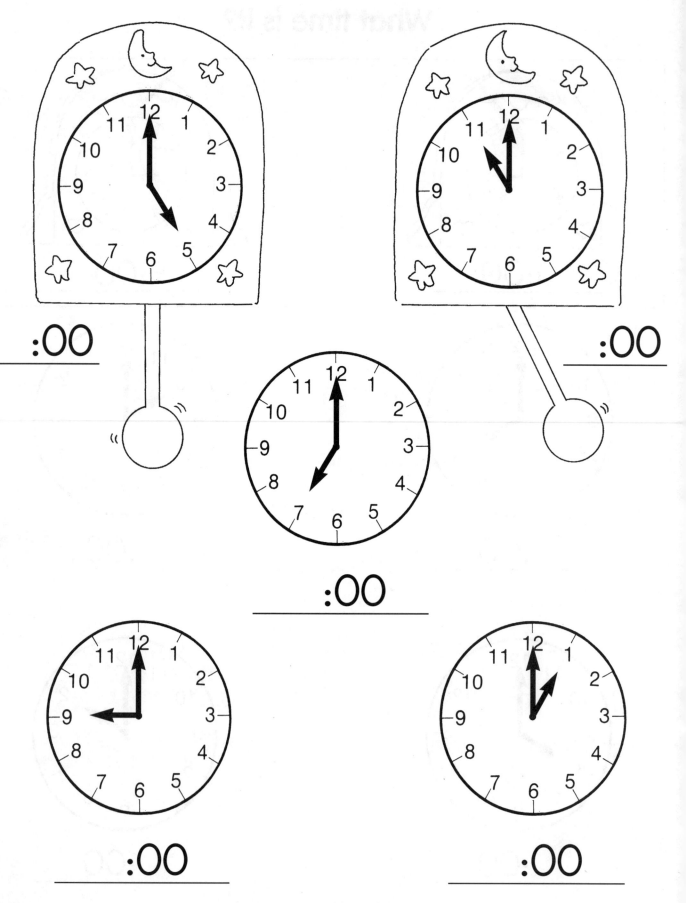

:00

:00

:00

:00

:00

Telling time to the hour; writing time

Write the numbers on the clock.

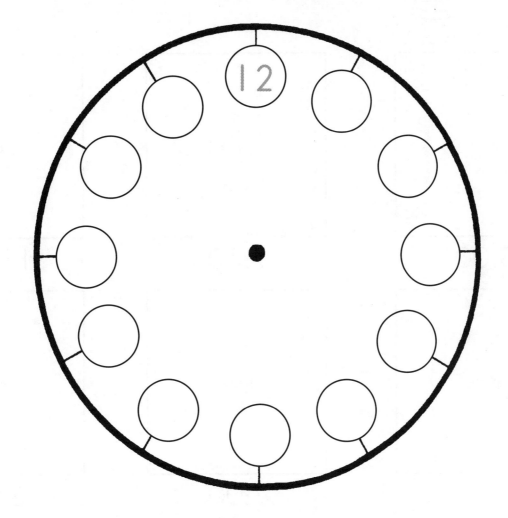

What time is it?

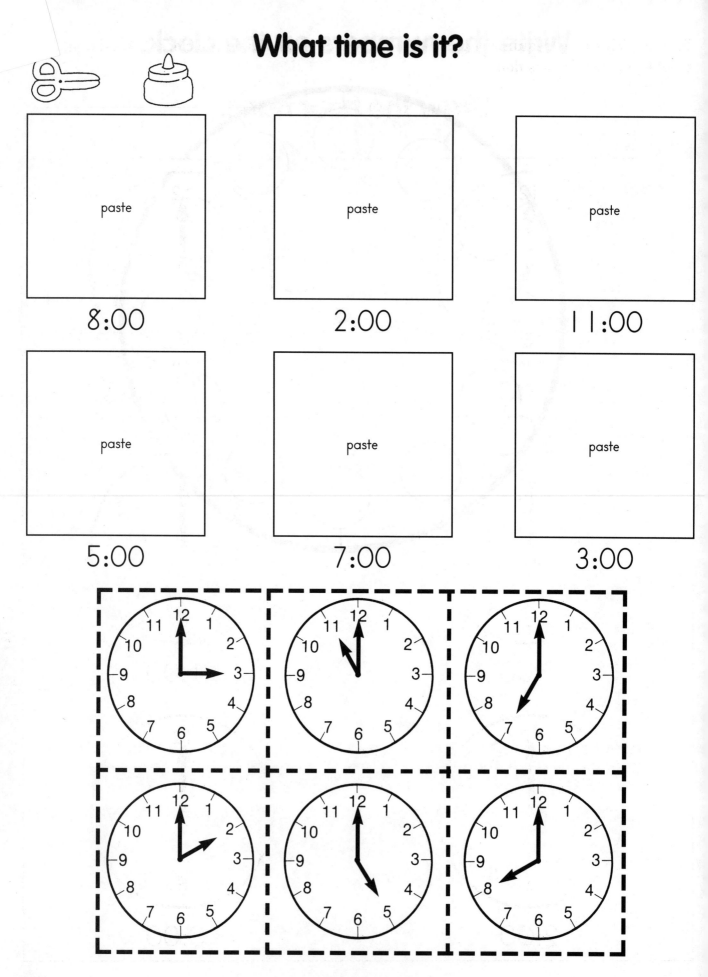

paste	paste	paste
8:00	2:00	11:00

paste	paste	paste
5:00	7:00	3:00

Matching clock time with written time

Parents: This page requires your child to draw the hour hand on the clock. If he/she has trouble, show how it is done.

Draw the hour hand.

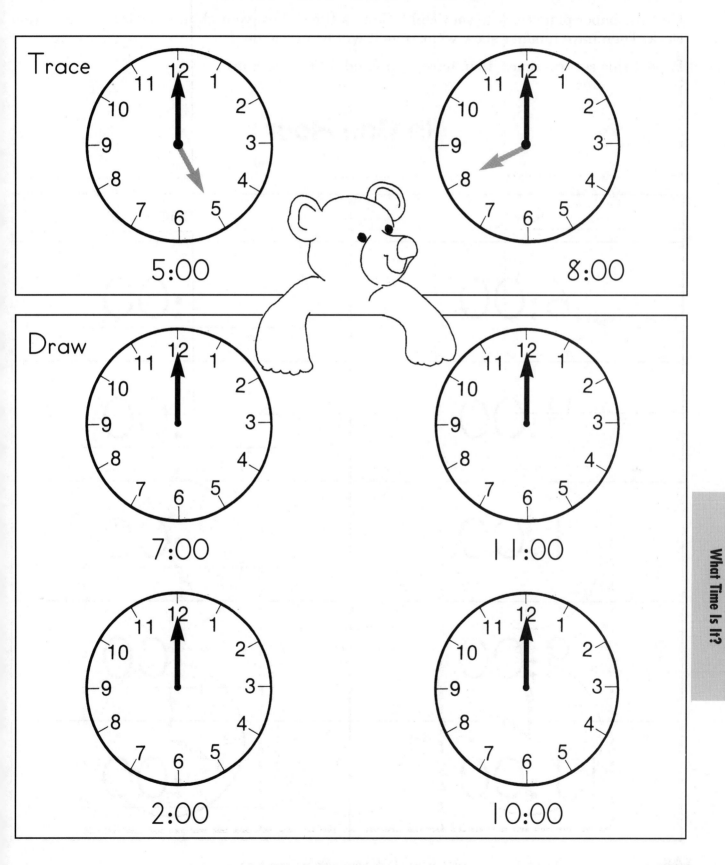

Trace

5:00

8:00

Draw

7:00

11:00

2:00

10:00

Parents:

Use the paper plate clock to show how time changes. Put a time on the clock and say "Now it is 3 o'clock ." In one hour it will be 4 o'clock ." Repeat this several times showing different hours.

Give the paper plate clock to your child. State a time. Have your child show that time on the clock. Then have him/her show what time it will be in one hour.

Repeat this several times, then have your child fill in this chart.

In One Hour

now	in one hour
6:00	____ :00
4:00	____ :00
1:00	____ :00
9:00	____ :00
11:00	____ :00

Understanding one hour later; writing time

Parents: Certain times are tricky to read when you are just learning. Show your child how the hands look on a clock at 6:00 and at 12:00.

6 o'clock or 12 o'clock?

Draw on the hands.

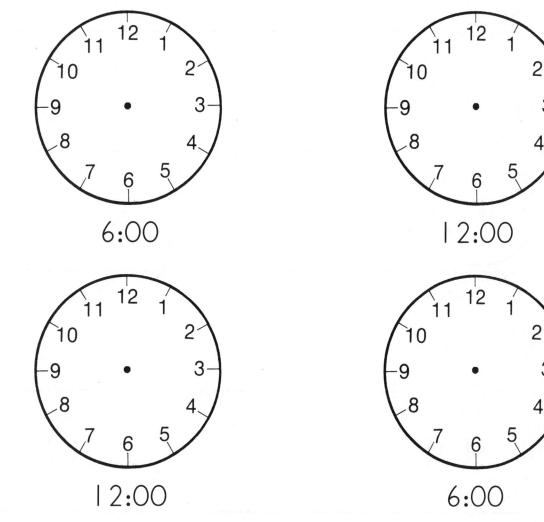

6:00

12:00

12:00

6:00

Drawing hour and minute hands to show time

What Time Is It?

111

Parents: Help your child keep this chart for one day. Choose any day your child is not in school. As much as possible, stop each hour to have your child read the hour and write down what he/she is doing. If your child is not writing, have him/her draw a picture instead.

What I Did Today

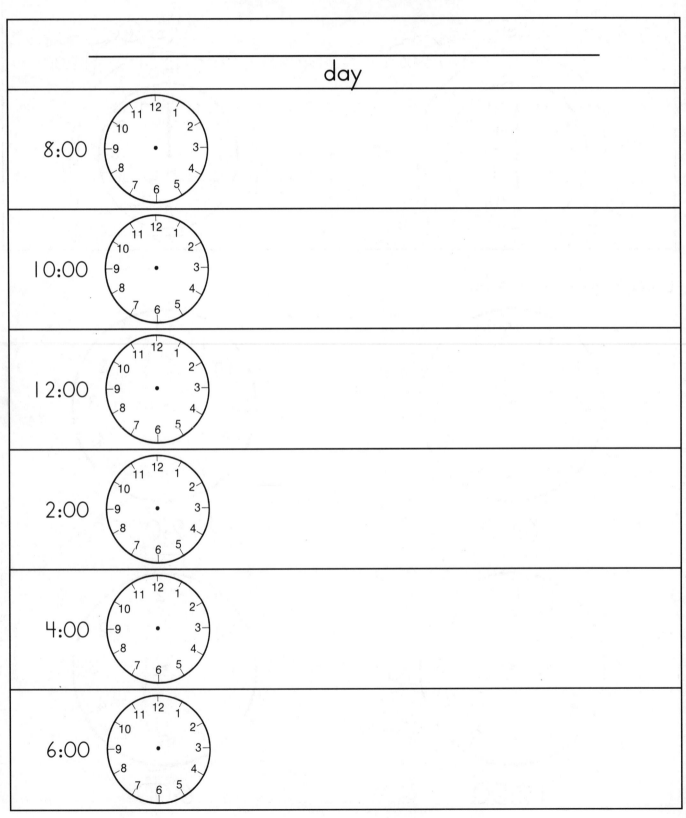

day

8:00

10:00

12:00

2:00

4:00

6:00

Drawing hour and minute hands to show time

Half-Past the Hour

Parents:

When your child is comfortable reading time to the hour, use the paper plate clock to show where the big hand is when it is a half hour (on the six).

Show where the hour hand is (between two numbers). Explain that you say "half past" and give the number.

Have your child move the minute hand to the six. Then have him/her move the hour hand half-way past a number and tell you the time. Prompt your child to say "It is half-past
_____(time)_____."

Repeat the activity several times, then have your child look at these clocks and tell you the time.

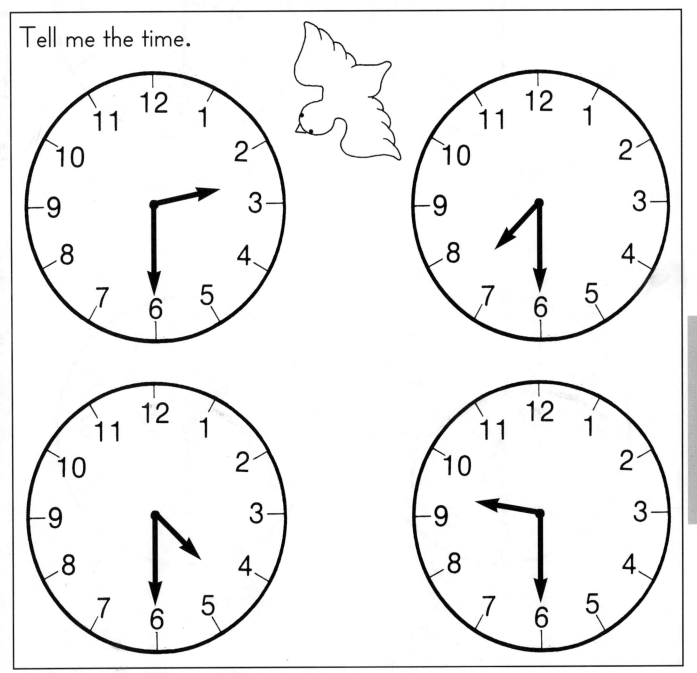

Tell me the time.

Parents: Explain to your child that there is another way to say a time like "half-past four."
We can also say "4:30." They both mean the same time.

Fill in the Time

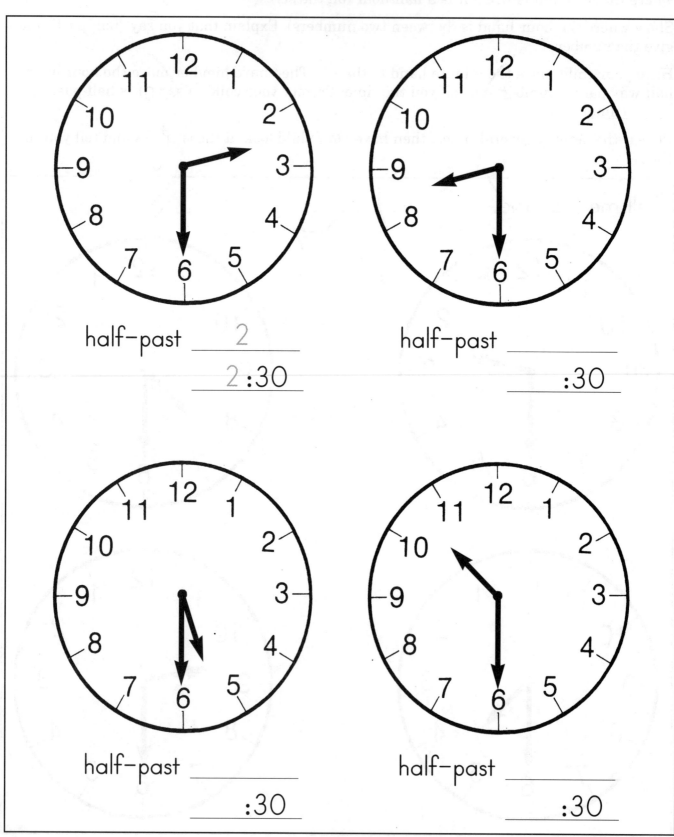

half-past _____2_____

_____2_____:30

half-past _____

_____:30

half-past _____

_____:30

half-past _____

_____:30

Telling time to the half-hour; writing time

What time is it?

4:30

7:30

2:30

5:30

1:30

9:30

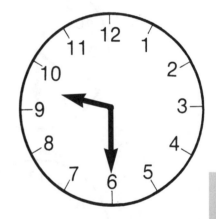

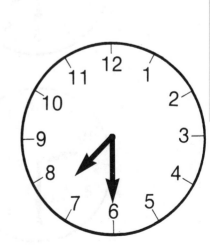

Parents: Explain to your child that clocks come in two different kinds. Some use hands (traditional), others show the numbers (digital).

Two Kinds of Clocks

Match:

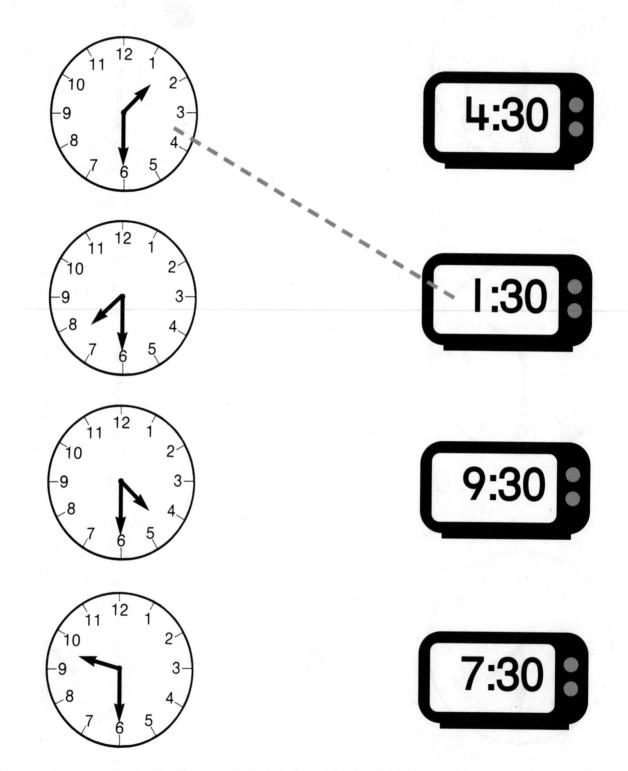

Matching times on digital and traditional clocks

Where does the little hand go?

2:30

8:30

3:30

7:30

9:30

4:30

Drawing in the hour hand to show time

Half-past the Hour

Circle the time.

4:30

(2:30)

12:30

8:30

11:30

7:30

2:30

4:30

7:30

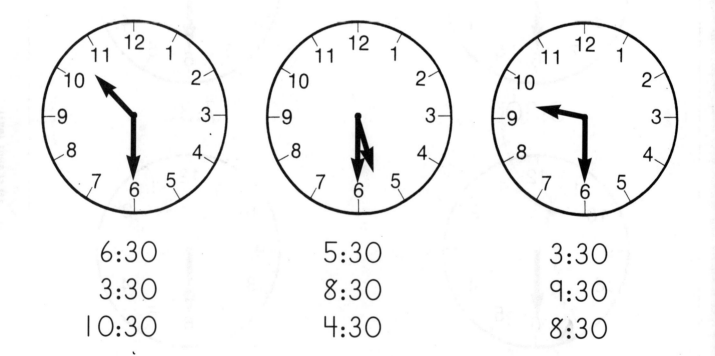

6:30

3:30

10:30

5:30

8:30

4:30

3:30

9:30

8:30

Telling time to the half-hour

What Time Is It?

Circle the time.

9:30
(4:30)
6:30

2:30
7:30
1:30

8:30
5:30
9:30

7:30
2:30
4:30

10:30
9:30
11:30

12:30
5:30
1:30

What time is it?

Match.

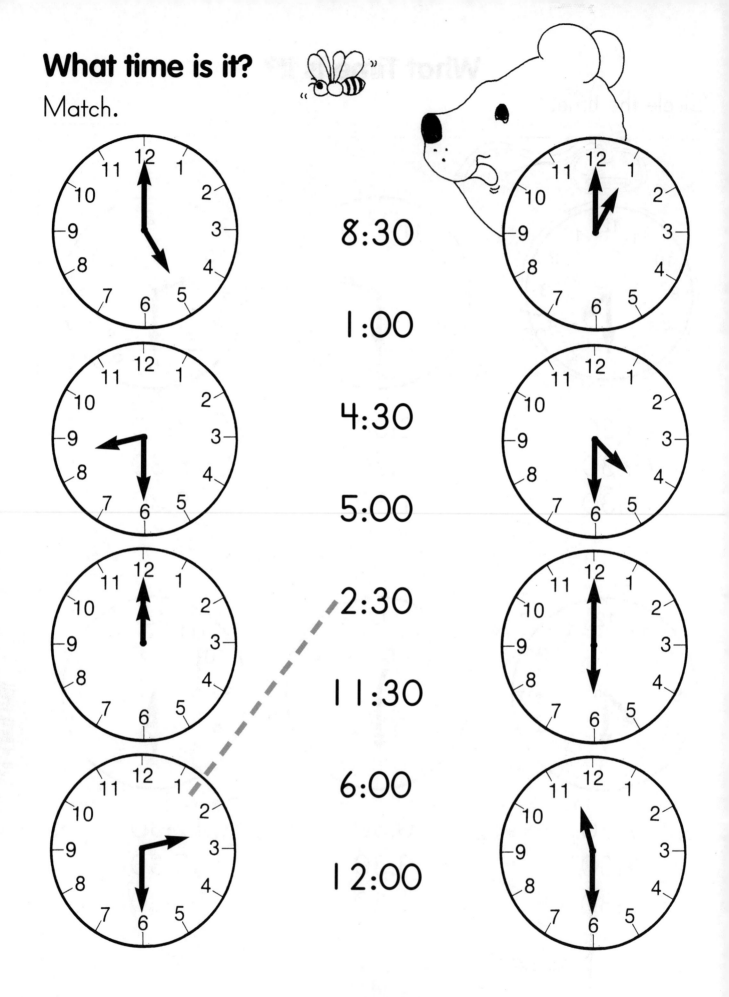

8:30

1:00

4:30

5:00

2:30

11:30

6:00

12:00

Telling time to the hour and half-hour

What time is it?

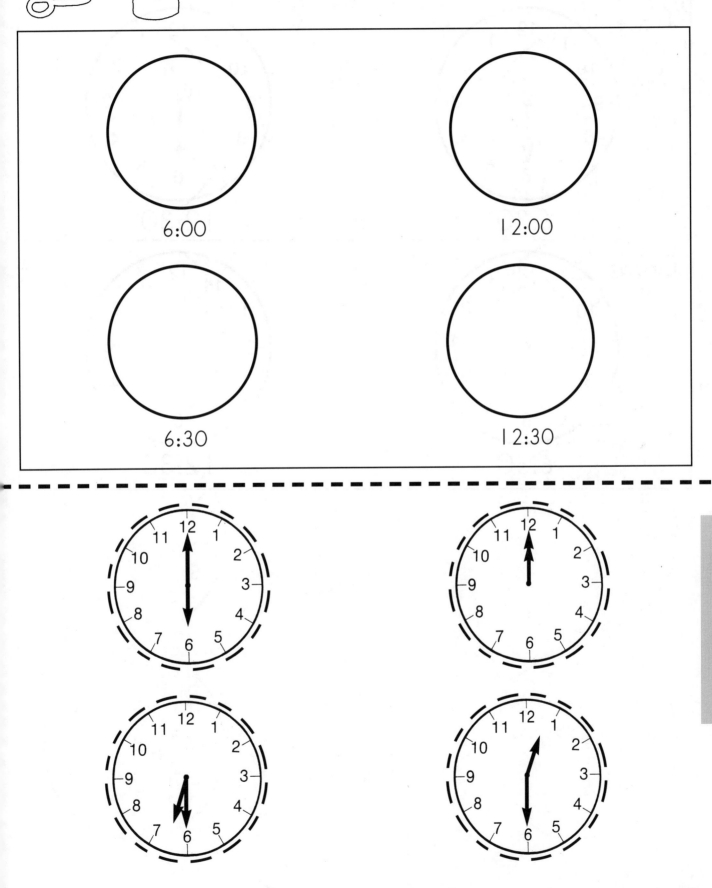

6:00

12:00

6:30

12:30

Put the hands on the clocks.

Trace

6:30

12:30

Draw

6:30

12:30

Drawing hour and minute hands to show time

Match the Clocks

2:00

4:30

6:00

8:30

10:30

12:00

Matching times on digital and traditional clocks

Parents: Help your child fill in the times on this bedtime chart. Keep the chart for one week.

_____'s Bedtime Chart

childs name

Day	Time
Saturday	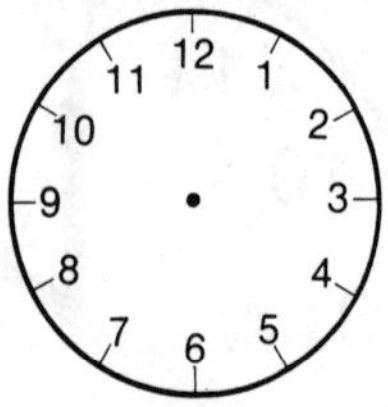
Sunday	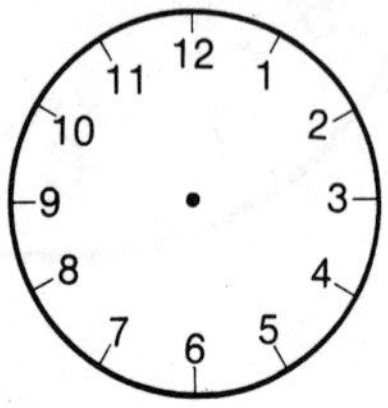
Monday	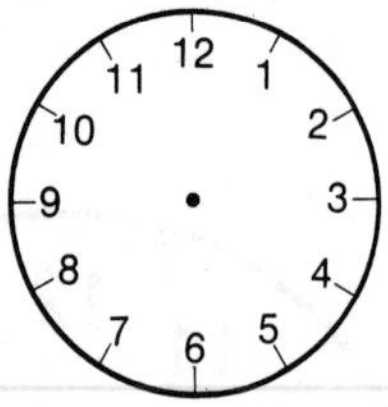
Tuesday	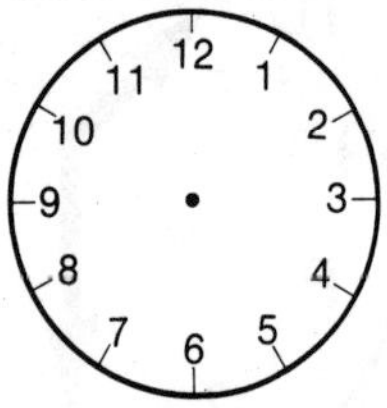
Wednesday	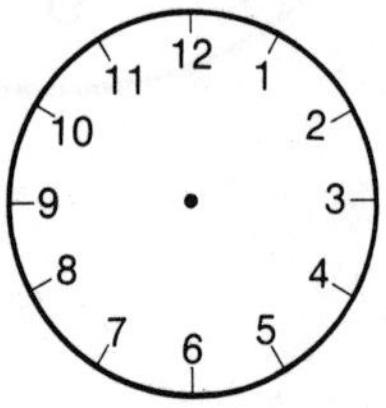
Thursday	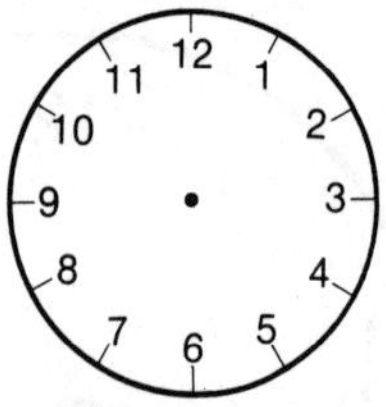
Friday	

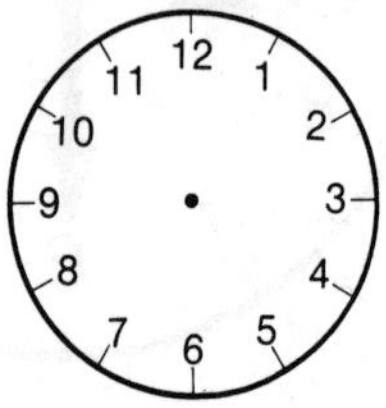

Drawing hour and minute hands

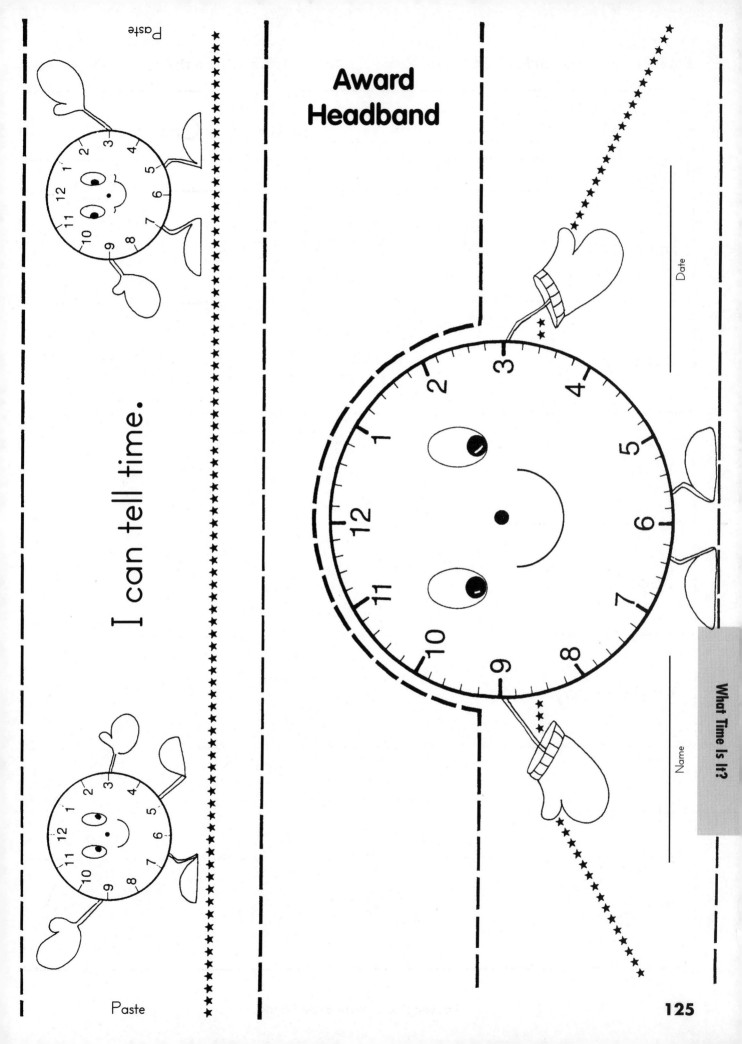

Award
Headband

I can tell time.

Paste

Paste

Paste

What Time Is It?

Name

Date

125

Answer Key

Please take time to go over the work your child has completed. Ask your child to explain what he/she has done. Praise both success and effort. If mistakes have been made, explain what the answer should have been and how to find it. Let your child know that mistakes are a part of learning. The time you spend with your child helps let him/her know you feel learning is important.

page 101

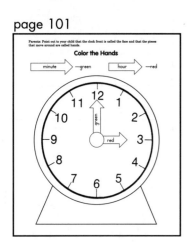

page 103

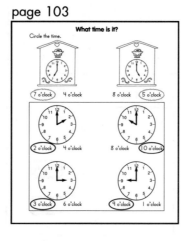

page 104

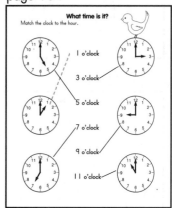

page 105

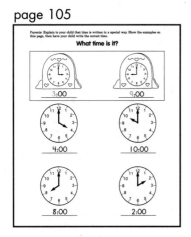

page 106

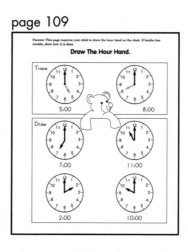

page 107

Write the numbers on the clock.

page 108

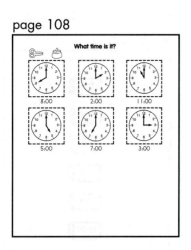

page 109

Draw The Hour Hand.

page 110

In One Hour

now	in one hour
6:00	7:00
4:00	5:00
1:00	2:00
9:00	10:00
11:00	12:00

page 111

Parents: Certain times are tricky to read when you are just learning. Show your child how the hands look on a clock at 6:00 and at 12:00.

6 o'clock or 12 o'clock?

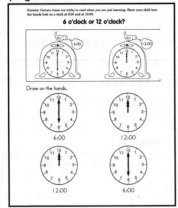

Draw on the hands.

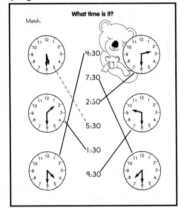

6:00   12:00

12:00   6:00

page 112

Parents: Help your child keep this chart for one day. Choose any day your child is not in school. As much as possible, stop each hour to have your child read the hour and write down what he/she is doing. If your child is not writing, have him/her draw a picture instead.

What I Did Today

_____ day

8:00   answers will vary

10:00

12:00

2:00

4:00

6:00

page 114

Parents: Explain to your child that there is another way to say a time like "half-past four." We can also say "4:30." They both mean the same time.

Fill in the Time

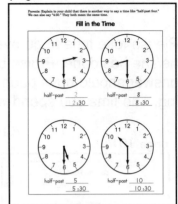

half-past   2   half-past   8
      2:30   8:30

half-past   5   half-past   10
      5:30   10:30

page 115

What time is it?

Match.

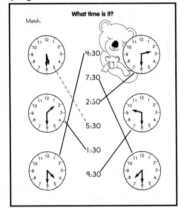

4:30
7:30
2:30
5:30
1:30
9:30

page 116

Parents: Explain to your child that clocks come in two different kinds. Some use hands (traditional), others show the numbers (digital).

Two Kinds of Clocks

Match:

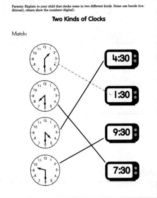

4:30
1:30
9:30
7:30

page 117

Where does the little hand go?

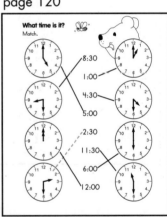

2:30   8:30

3:30   7:30

9:30   4:30

page 118

Half-past the Hour

Circle the time.

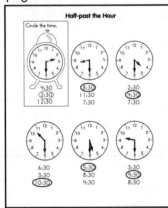

4:30   8:30   2:30
(2:30)   11:30   (4:30)
12:30   7:30   7:30

6:30   (5:30)   3:30
3:30   8:30   (9:30)
(10:30) 4:30   8:30

page 119

What Time Is It?

Circle the time.

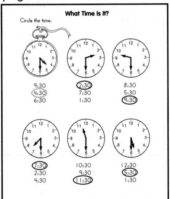

9:30   (2:30)   8:30
(4:30)   7:30   5:30
6:30   1:30   (1:30)

(7:30)   10:30   12:30
2:30   9:30   (5:30)
4:30   (11:30) 1:30

page 120

What time is it?

Match.

8:30
1:00
4:30
5:00
2:30
11:30
6:00
12:00

page 121

What time is it?

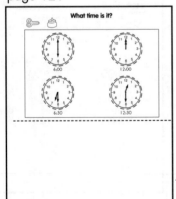

6:00   12:00

6:30   12:30

page 122

Put the hands on the clocks.

Trace

6:30   12:30

Draw

6:30   12:30

page 123

Match the Clocks

2:00
4:30
6:00
8:30
10:30
12:00

128   Answers

Reviewing Kindergarten

One of the best ways to check your child's mathematics knowledge and skills is to observe him/her in everyday life. Watch to see if your child:

- notices numbers in the world around him/her
- counts objects or counts in sequence
- uses comparing words (biggest, most, etc.) as he/she talks
- shares items evenly with friends (one for you and one for me)
- notices time
- recognizes money and understands it has value

Checking math skills

Parents: Point out a few objects around the house. Ask you child to tell you which one is the largest and which is the smallest.

Skill: can identify objects and make comparisons
using descriptive language - largest, smallest

Color the largest ball green.
Color the smallest ball red.

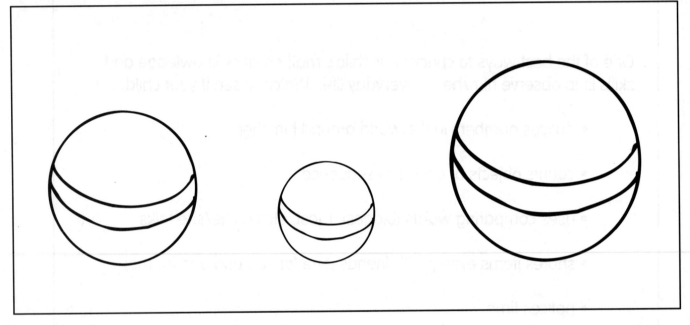

Color the largest flower orange.
Put an X on the smallest flower.

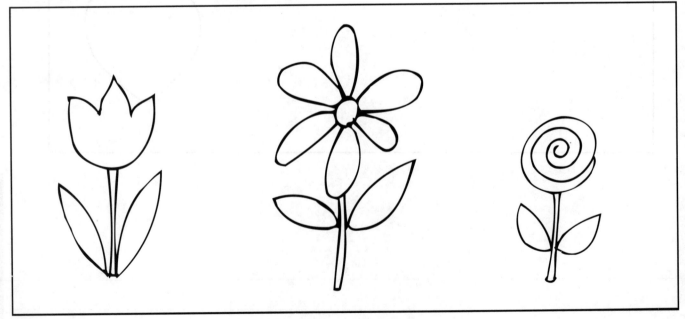

Parents: Show your child three shoes of different sizes. Ask him/her to tell you which one is the longest and which is the shortest.

Skill: can identify objects and make comparisons using descriptive language - longest, shortest

Circle the longest caterpillar.
Put an X on the shortest caterpillar.

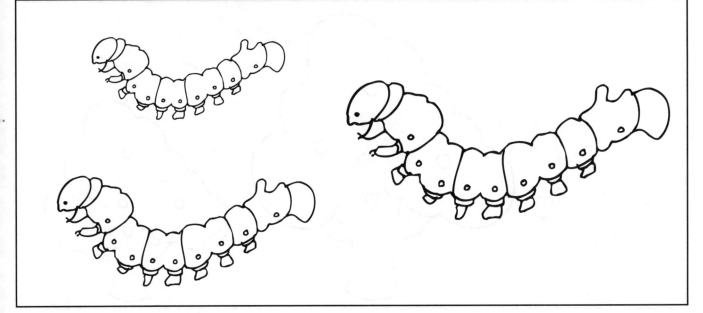

Color the longest boat red.
Color the shortest boat yellow.

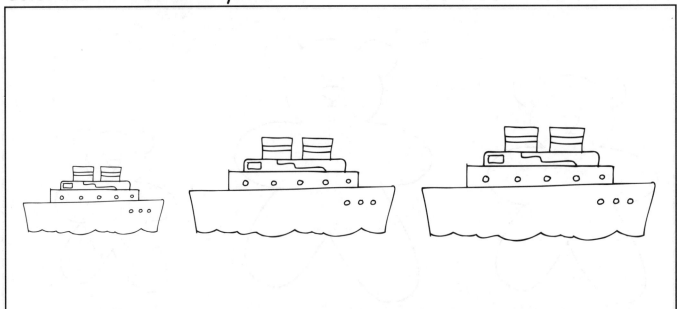

Comparing length

Parents: Stand next to your child. Ask him/her to tell you who is taller and who is shorter.

Skill: can identify objects and make comparisons
using descriptive language - shortest, tallest

Color the tallest tree green.
Put an X on the shortest tree.

Put an X on the tallest bear.
Color the smallest bear brown.

Parents: Guide your child through the steps to make this "monkey on a stick," then do the position activities with him/her.

Skill: • understands about the relative position of things
• uses the correct terms for locations
(above, under, right, behind, etc.)

Make the Monkey:
Cut out the monkey pattern.
Tape or glue it to the end of an ice cream stick or ruler.

Play "Where is the Monkey?"
Place the monkey somewhere around your body and ask your child "Where is the monkey?" Listen to his/her response.

- behind your back
- between your knees
- over your head

- in front of your chest
- next to your shoulder
- etc.

Play "Show Me."
Give the monkey to your child. Ask him/her to put the monkey where you say.

- under your chin
- over you head

- behind your feet
- etc.

Understanding position words

With Your Child

Give your child a direction involving the use of positional words. Observe your child to see which words he/she understands. This observation can take place as you are doing other things together. Here are some directions you might use.

- Please put this book on the table.

- Take the newspaper and put it in the recycling bin.

- Put your slippers next to your bed.

- See it the dog is under the table.

- Come sit between us.

- Put a big spoon in the spaghetti bowl.

- Hang your coat on the bottom hook.

- Set your piggy bank on the top shelf.

Where Do the Monkeys Go?

on the rock

in the tub

under the tree

between the bananas

Cut out the monkeys.

Kindergarten Math

Parents: Your child needs to cut out the pictures on page 137. He/She will use the pictures to copy and complete the patterns below.

Skill: recognizes a pattern

Cut and paste. Copy the pattern.

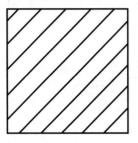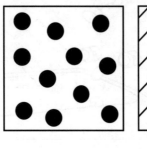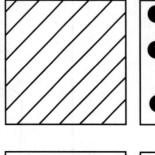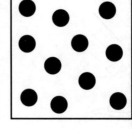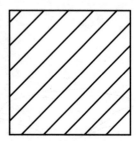

What comes next?

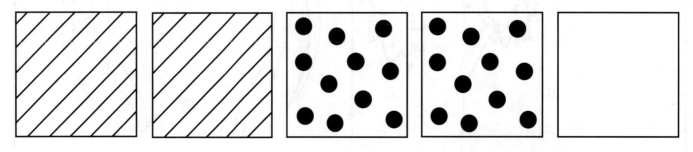

Completing patterns

Parents: Your child needs to cut out these pictures to use for patterning on page 136.

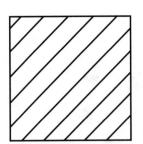 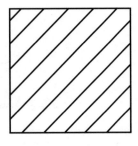 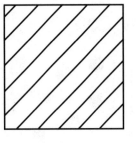

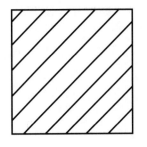 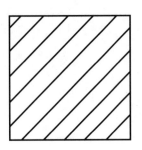 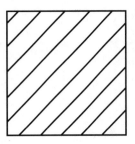

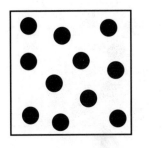 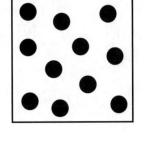 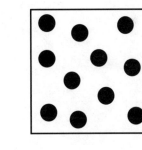

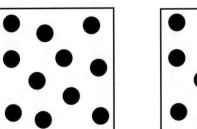 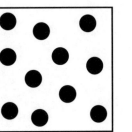 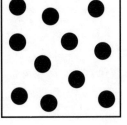

Completing patterns

Comparing patterns

Skill: identifies equivalent sets by one-to-one matching

Do you have a bone for every dog?
Match to find out.

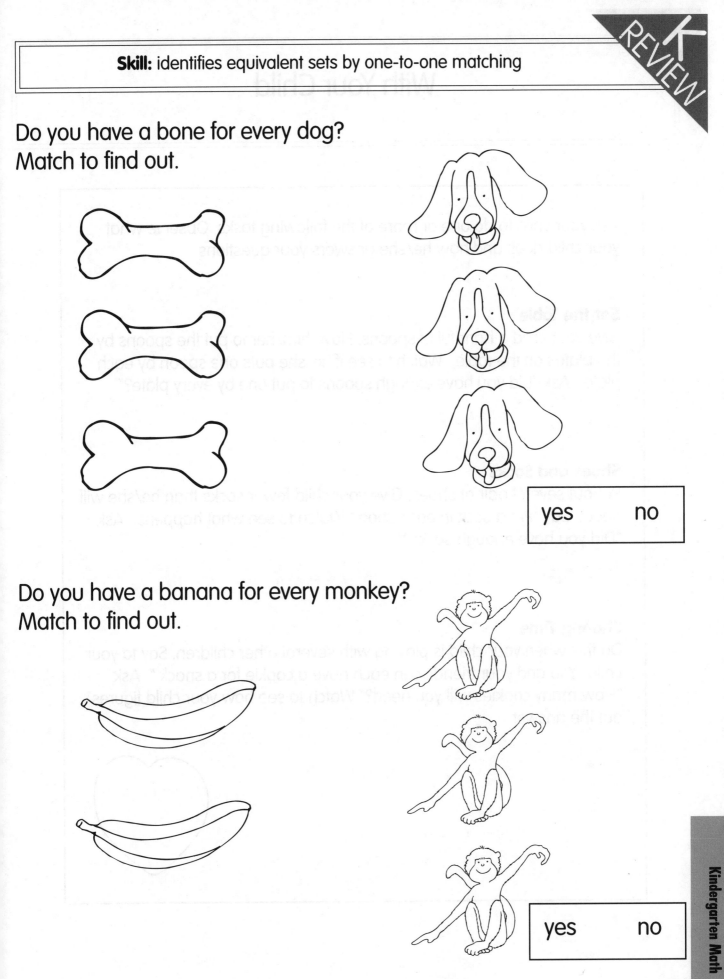

yes   no

Do you have a banana for every monkey?
Match to find out.

yes   no

With Your Child

Ask your child to do one or more of the following tasks. Observe what your child does and how he/she answers your questions.

Set the Table
Give your child a handful of spoons. Have him/her to put the spoons by the plates on the table. Watch to see if he/she puts one spoon by each plate. Ask "Did you have enough spoons to put one by every plate?"

Shoes and Socks
Put out several pair of shoes. Give your child fewer socks than he/she will need. Say "Put a sock in each shoe." Watch to see what happens. Ask "Did you have enough socks?"

Sharing Time
Do this when your child is playing with several other children. Say to your child "You and your friends can each have a cookie for a snack." Ask "How many cookies will you need?" Watch to see how your child figures out the answer.

Parents: Have your child count each set of objects, then tell you how many there are.
Notice which amounts he/she recognizes by sight.

Skill: identifies sets of 1-5 objects

Count.

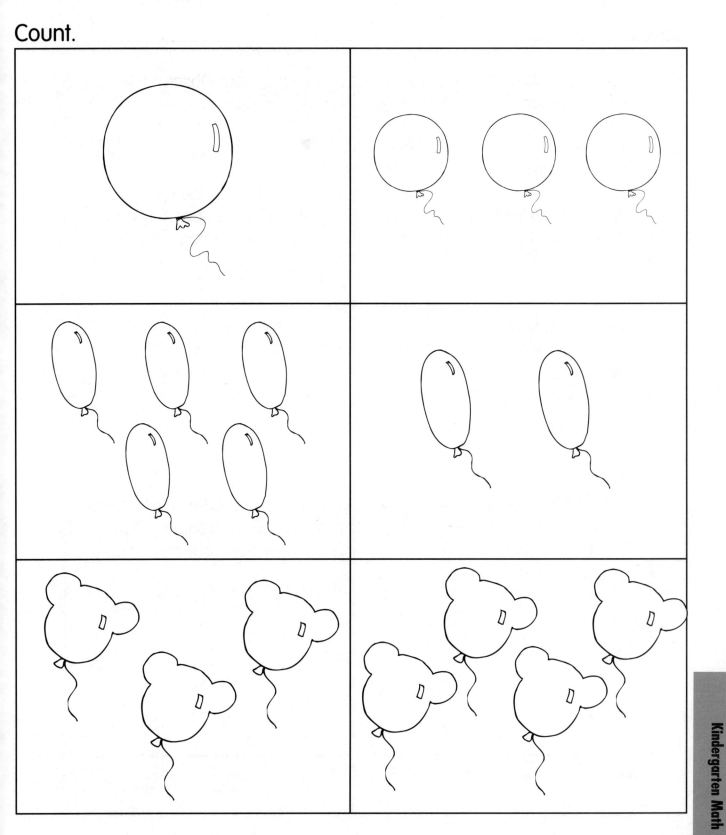

Kindergarten Math

Parents: Have your child count each set of objects, then tell you how many there are. Notice which amounts he/she recognizes by sight.

Skill: identifies sets of 6-10 objects

Count.

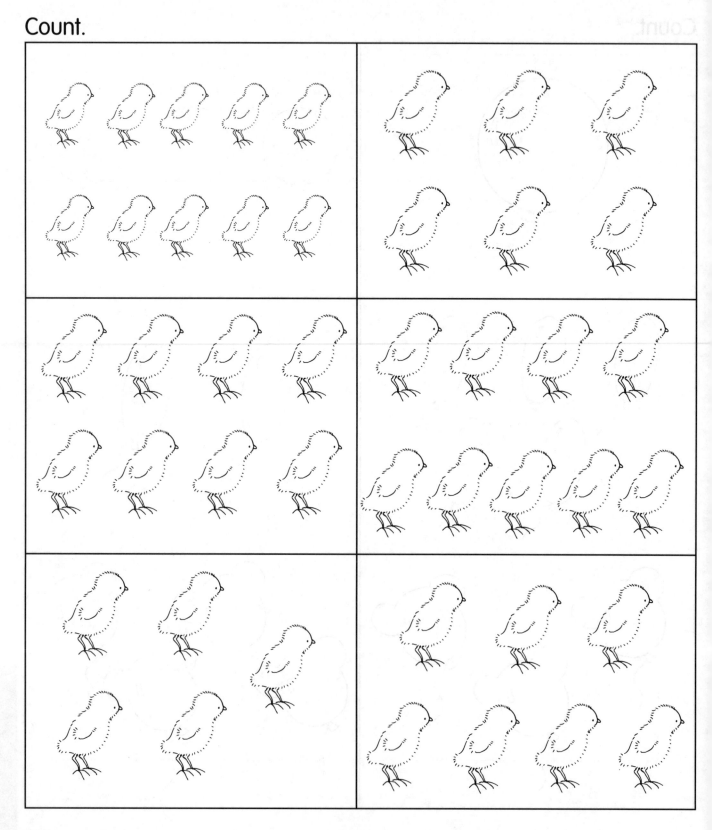

With Your Child

Ask your child to count objects around the house and in the yard. Observe how far and how accurate he/she can count.

- bags of leaves you have raked up
- cans of food for the pet cat or dog
- doors in the house
- wheels on a toy
- people in the family
- trees in your yard

Ask your child to bring you a specific number of items. For example:

- spoons to put on the table
- napkins for the table or lunch boxes
- oranges for lunch boxes
- envelopes for your letters or cards
- hangers for clothes coming out of the dryer
- flowers from the backyard for a bouquet
- potatoes to cook for dinner

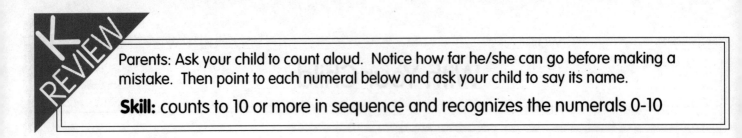

Parents: Ask your child to count aloud. Notice how far he/she can go before making a mistake. Then point to each numeral below and ask your child to say its name.

Skill: counts to 10 or more in sequence and recognizes the numerals 0-10

5   2   7

9   0   1

8   6   3

10   4

Skill: sequences numbers to 10

Help the monkey find its banana.

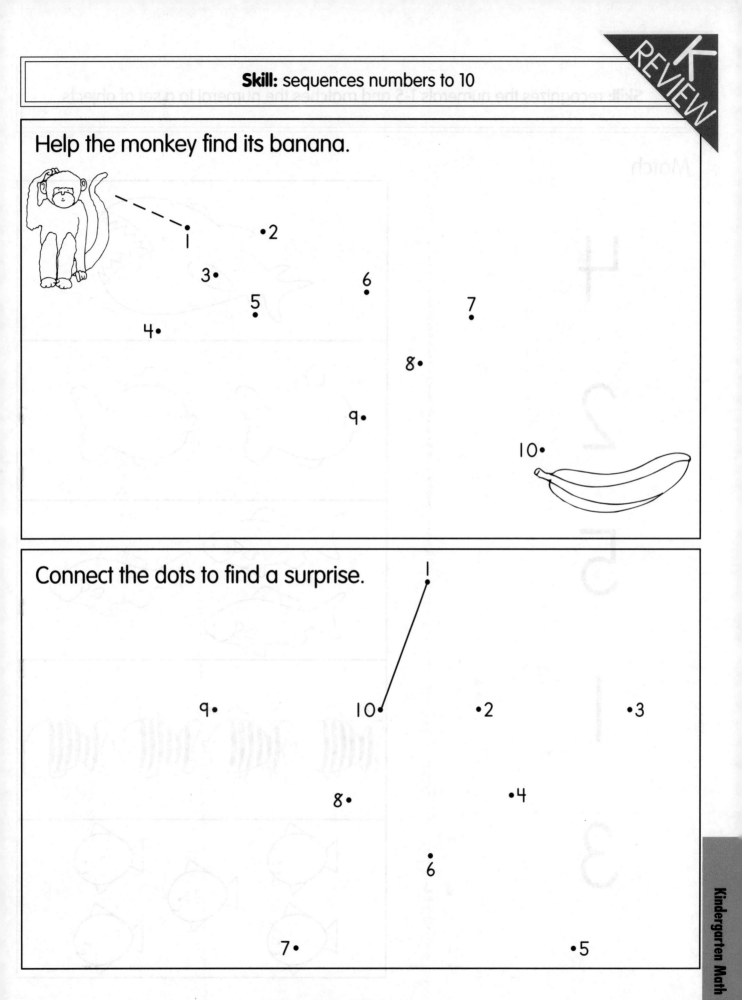

1
•2
3•
6
5
7
4•
8•
9•
10•

Connect the dots to find a surprise.

1
9•   10•   •2   •3
8•   •4
6
7•   •5

Understanding number order

Skill: recognizes the numerals 1-5 and matches the numeral to a set of objects

Match.

4

2

5

1

3

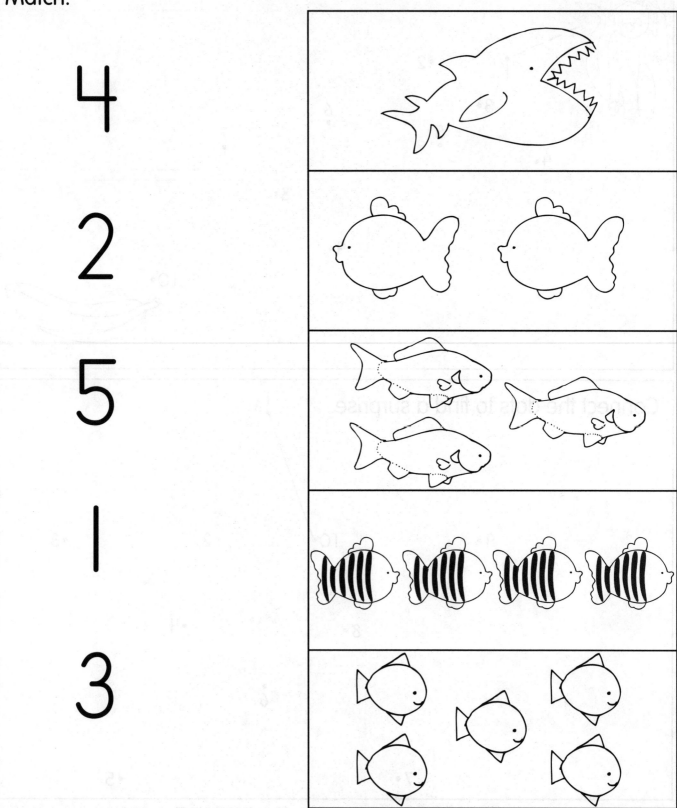

Counting objects and matching with a number

Skill: recognizes the numerals 6-10 and matches the numeral to a set of objects

Match.

7

10

6

9

8

Counting objects and matching with a number

Skill: can tell which of two sets contains more objects

Put an X on the box with more.

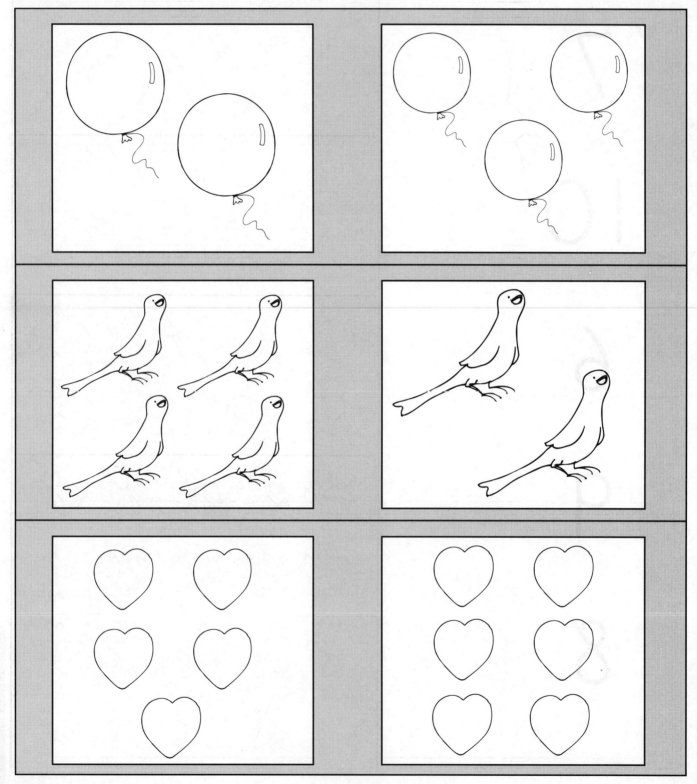

Understanding more and less

Skill: can tell which of two sets contains less objects

Put a circle around the box with less.

Understanding more and less

Kindergarten Math

Skill: can tell which of two numbers is less or more

Circle more.
Put an X on less.

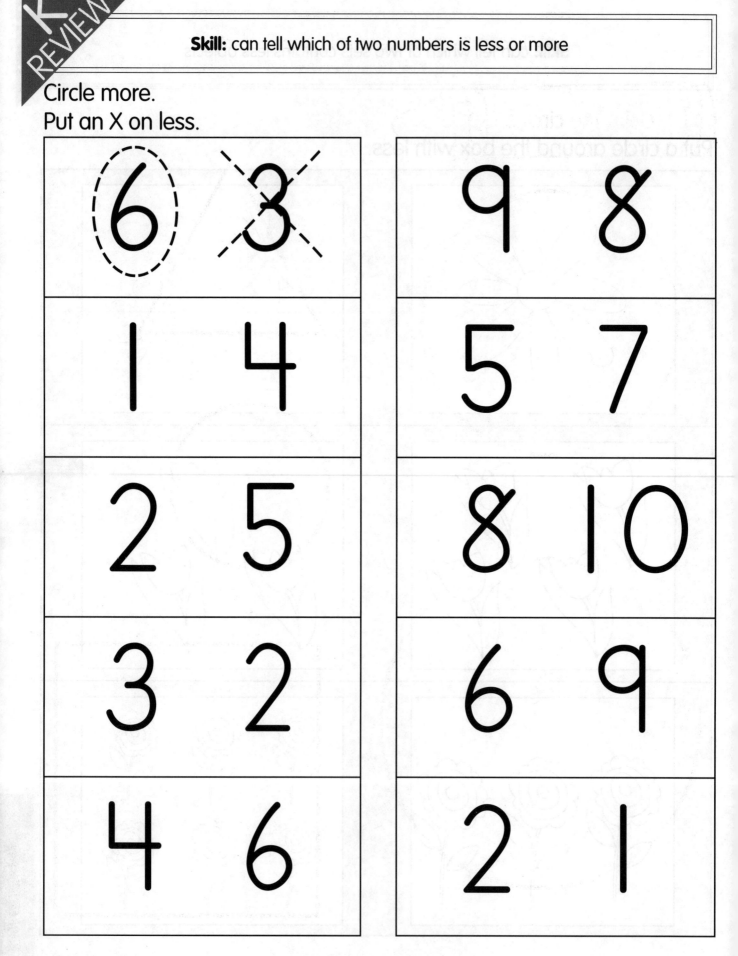

Understanding more and less

Skill: identifies basic geometric shapes - circle

Color the circles.

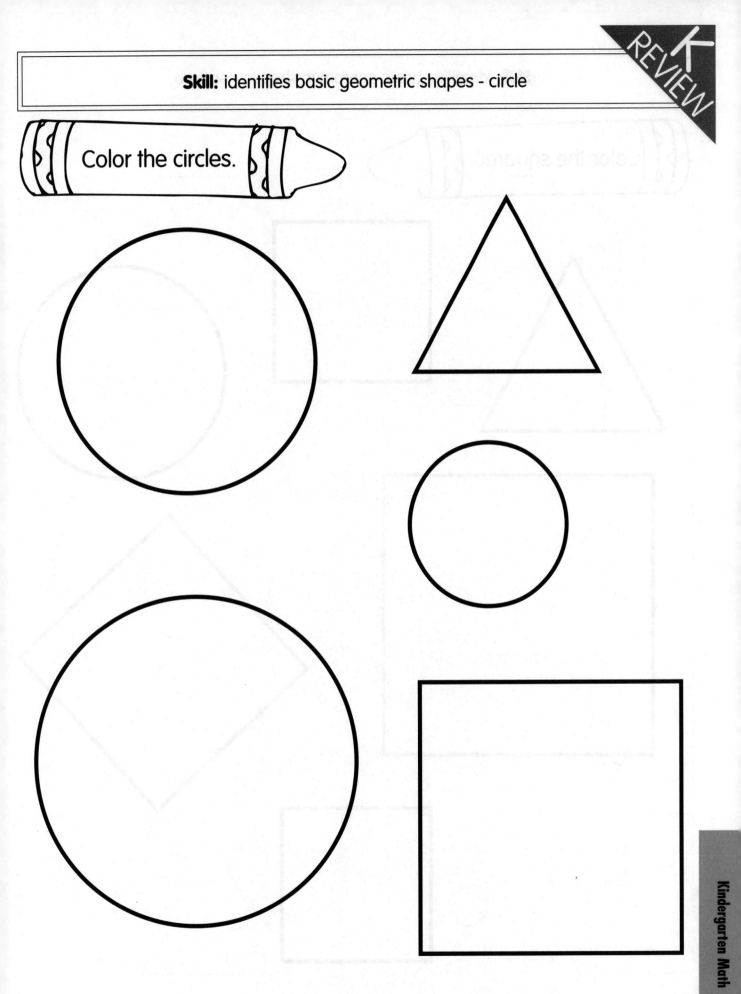

Recognizing shapes

Color the squares.

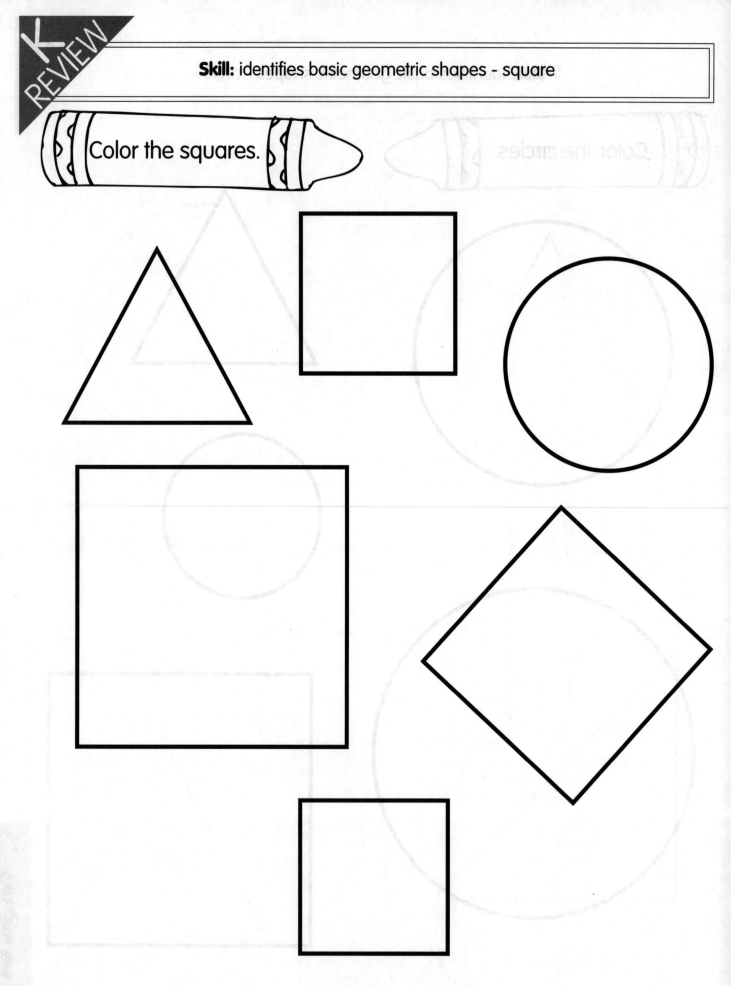

Recognizing shapes

Skill: identifies basic geometric shapes - triangles

Color the triangles.

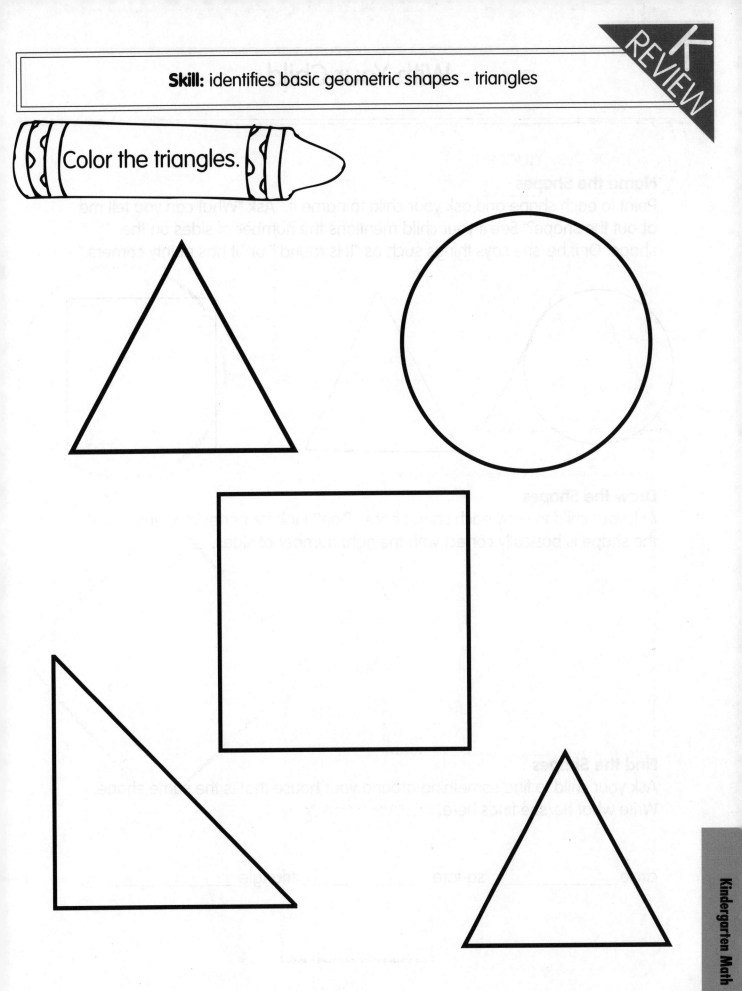

Recognizing shapes

153

With Your Child

Name the Shapes

Point to each shape and ask your child to name it. Ask "What can you tell me about the shape?" See if your child mentions the number of sides on the shape. Or if he/she says things such as "It is round." or "It has pointy corners."

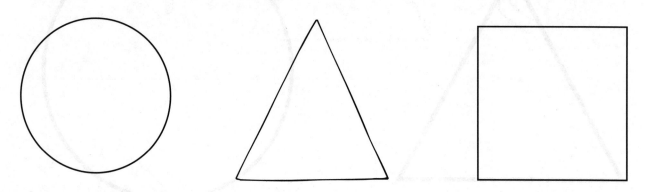

Draw the Shapes

Ask your child to copy each shape here. Don't look for perfection. Just see if the shape is basically correct with the right number of sides.

Find the Shapes

Ask your child to find something around your house that is the same shape. Write what he/she finds here.

circle _____ square _____ triangle _____

Skill: match the shapes

Matching shapes to real-life objects

Parents: Lay out a penny, nickel, and a dime. Ask your child to name each of the coins and to tell you how many cents it is.

Skill: • identifies and gives the value of coins

penny   nickel   dime

• figures the value of a group of coins when all are of the same type (example, all pennies)

How much money do you see?

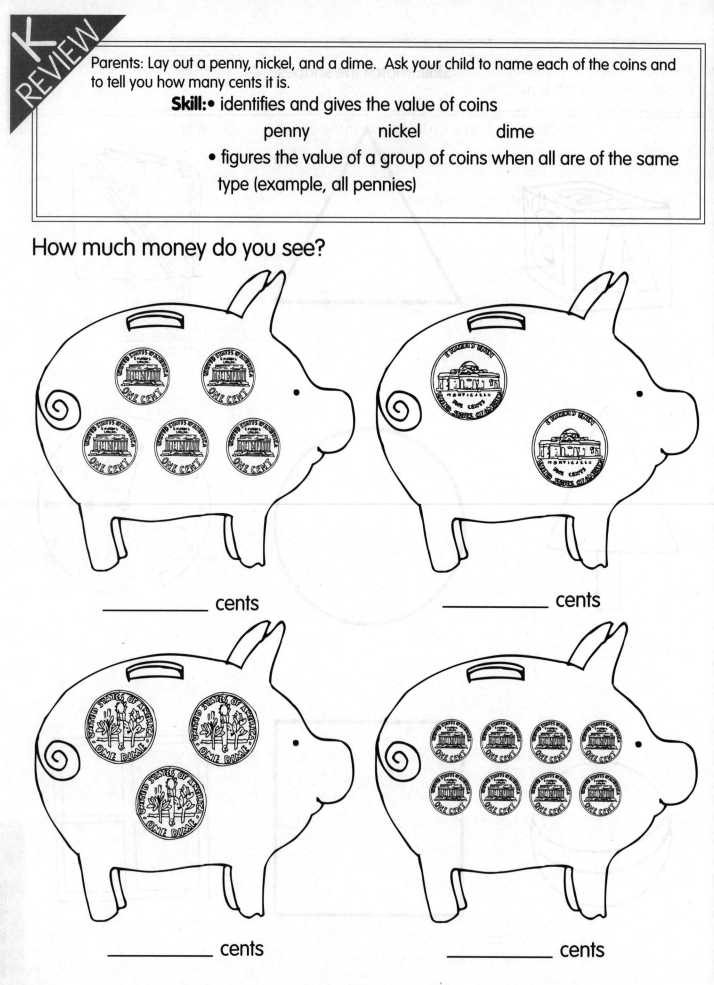

_____ cents

_____ cents

_____ cents

_____ cents

Counting change

Parents: Walk around the house and have your child point out the places that tell time. He/She doesn't need to read the timepiece, just identify it.

Skill: recognizes that clocks and watches measure time

Circle the things that tell time.

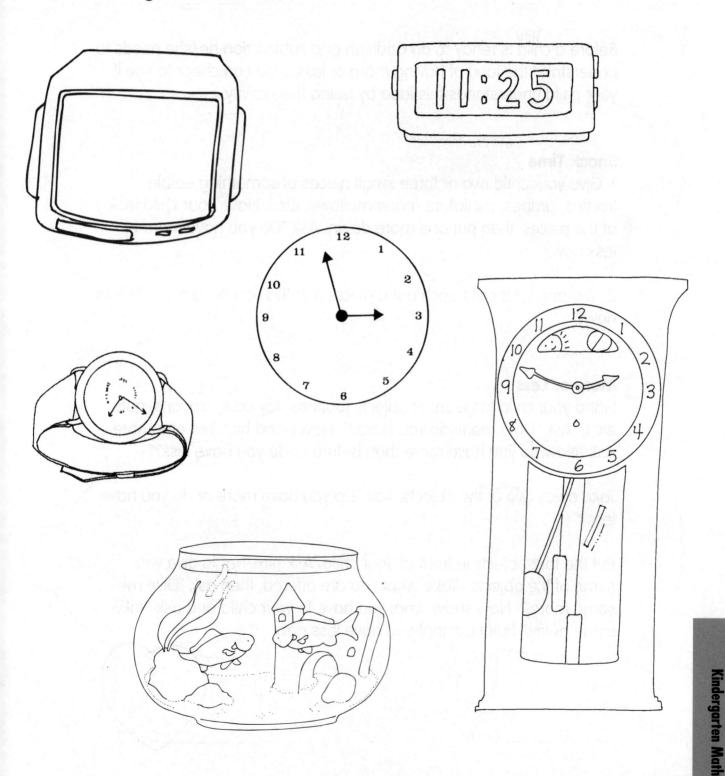

Recognizing clocks

Skill: understands that when objects are taken away you have less and objects are added you have more.

With Your Child

Before a child is ready to do addition and subtraction he/she needs to understand the idea of having more or less. You can check to see if your child understands this idea by doing this activity.

Snack Time
1. Give your child two or three small pieces of something edible (raisins, grapes, miniature marshmallows, etc.). Have your child look at the pieces, then put one more down. Ask "Do you have more or less now?"

2. You and your child each eat a piece. Ask "Do you have more or less now?"

More or Less
Hand your child three small objects (buttons, toy cars, crayons, nuts, etc.). Ask "How many do you have?" Now hand him/her one more. Ask "Now do you have more than before or do you have less?"

Take away two of the objects. Ask "Do you have more or do you have less?"

Put the four objects in front of your child. Ask him/her to give you some of the objects. Take what you are offered, then ask "Give me some more." Now show what you have to your child and ask "Take some away." Point out that you have less now.

Understanding more and less; add and take-away

Answer Key

Please take time to go over the work your child has completed. Ask your child to explain what he/she has done. Praise both success and effort. If mistakes have been made, explain what the answer should have been and how to find it. Let your child know that mistakes are a part of learning. The time you spend with your child helps let him/her know you feel learning is important.

page 130

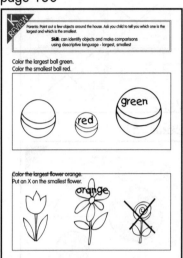

page 131

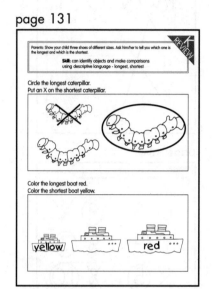

page 132

page 135

page 136

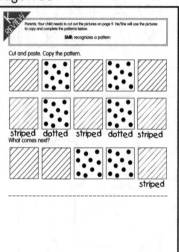

page 139

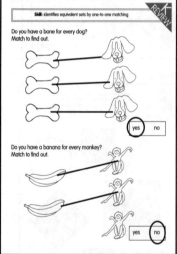

page 141

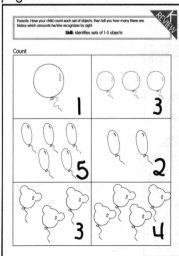

page 142

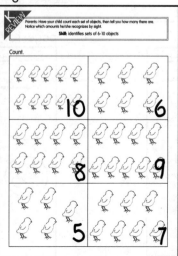

page 145

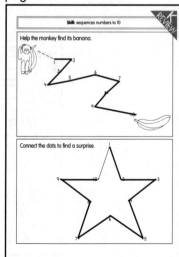

Kindergarten Math

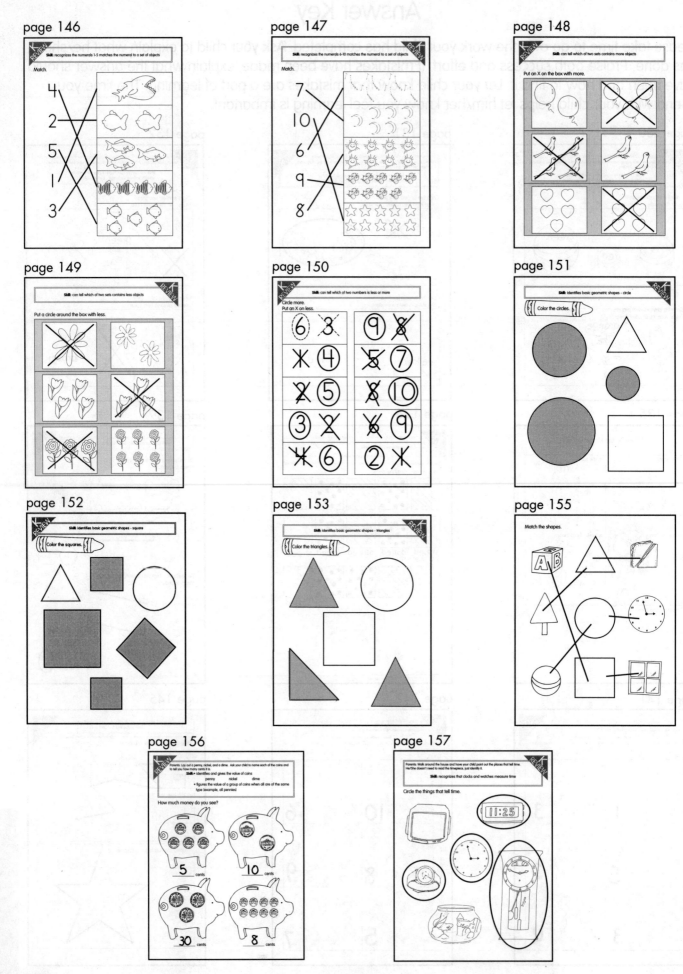

page 146

page 147

page 148

page 149

page 150

page 151

page 152

page 153

page 155

page 156

page 157

Basic Strokes

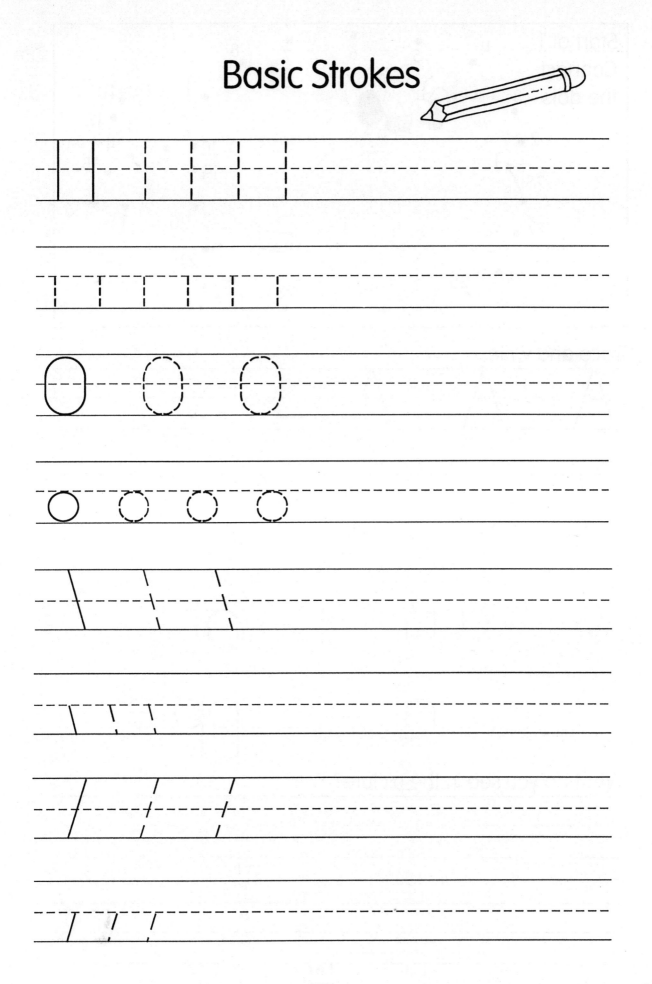

Start at 1.
Connect
the dots.

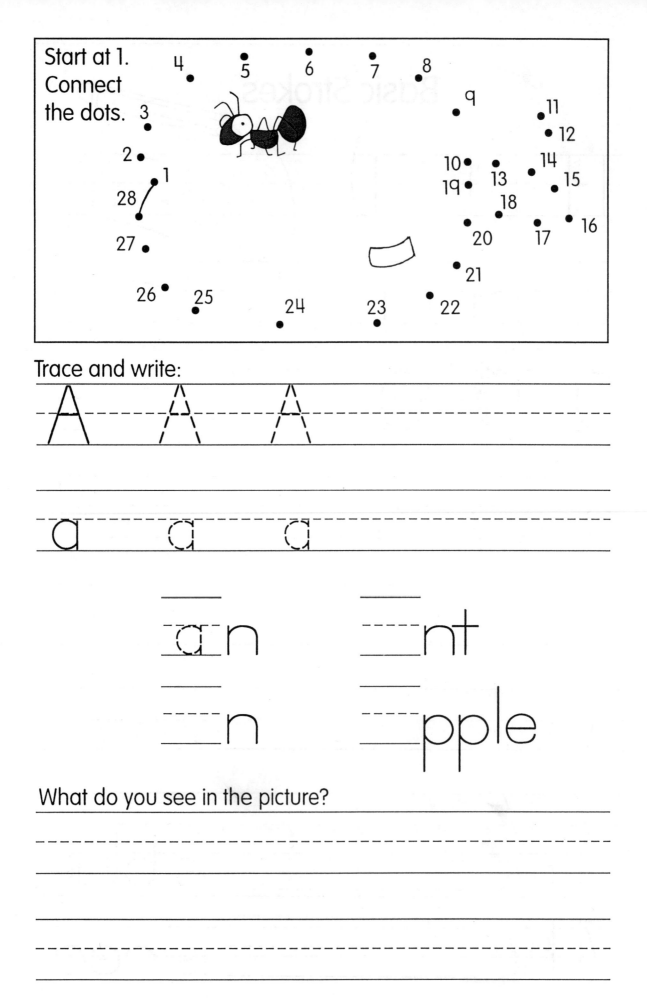

Trace and write:

A A A

a a a

an nt

n pple

What do you see in the picture?

Tracing and printing letters and words

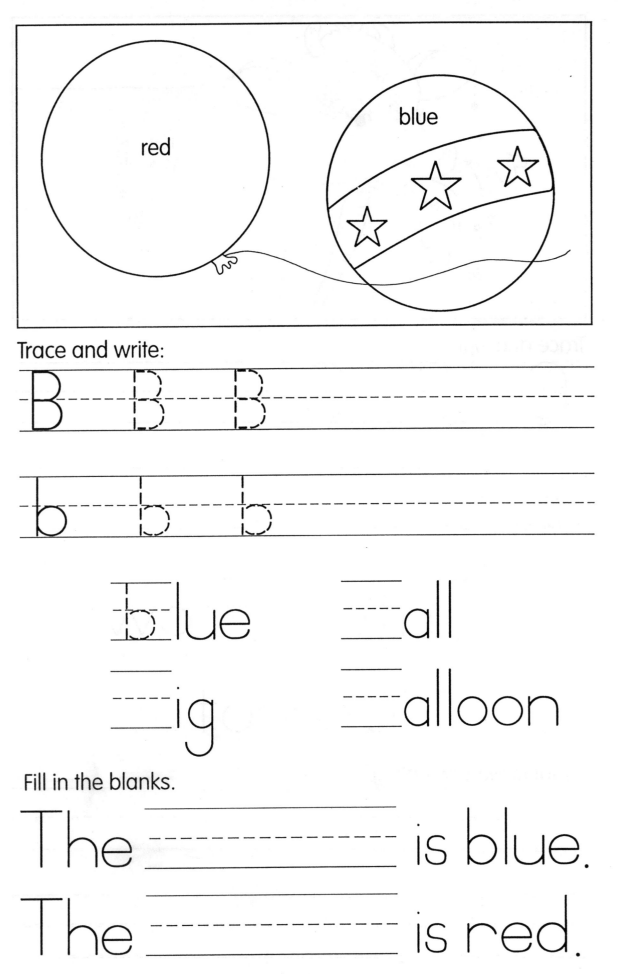

red

blue

Trace and write:

B B B

b b b

blue   all

ig   alloon

Fill in the blanks.

The _____ is blue.

The _____ is red.

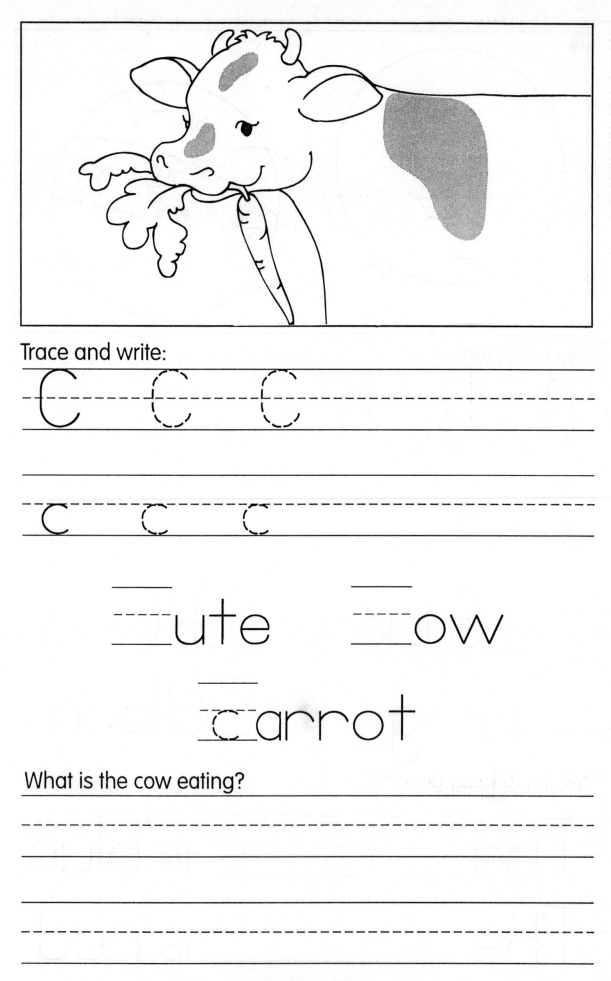

Trace and write:

C C C C

c c c c

Cute Cow

carrot

What is the cow eating?

_____

_____

_____

_____

Tracing and printing letters and words

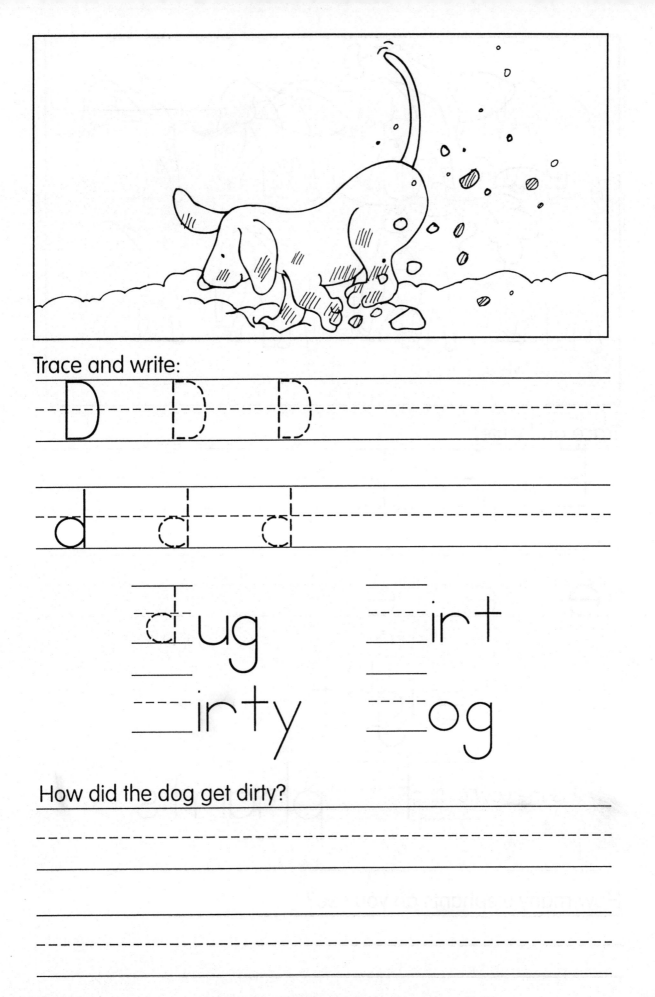

Trace and write:

D   D   D

d   d   d

dug   dirt

dirty   dog

How did the dog get dirty?

Tracing and printing letters and words   **165**

Trace and write:

E E E

e e e

eight

Elephants

How many elephants do you see?

Tracing and printing letters and words

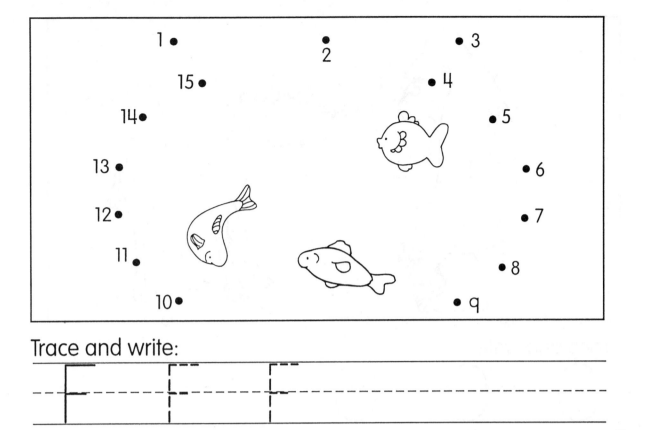

Trace and write:

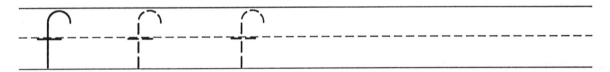

Fish

Funny

Make the fish in the fish bowl look funny.
Tell what you did.

Tracing and printing letters and words   **167**

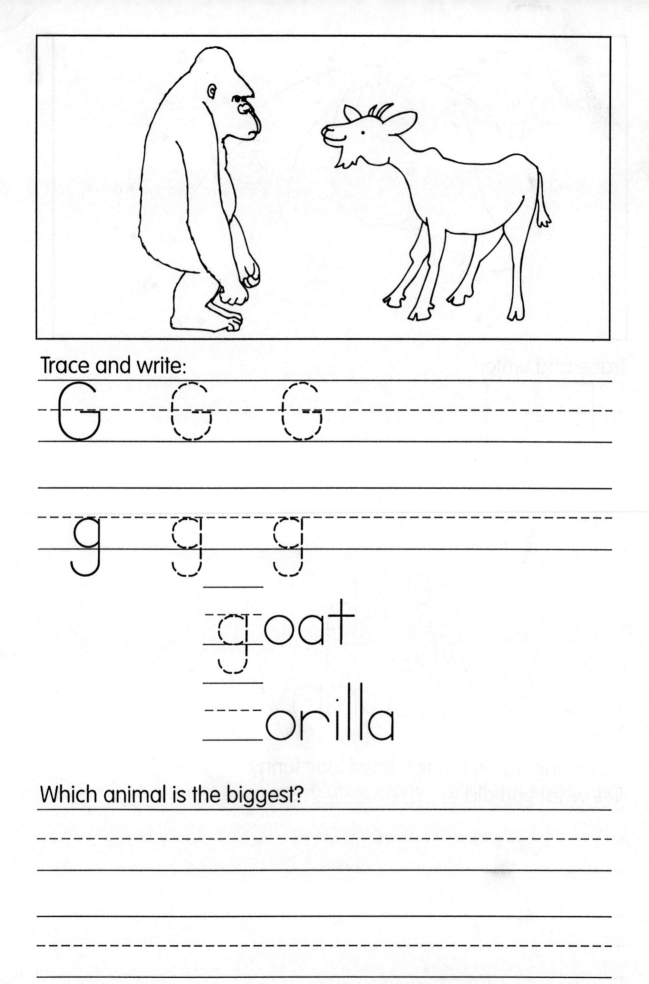

Trace and write:

G G G

g g g

goat

orilla

Which animal is the biggest?

Tracing and printing letters and words

Trace and write:

H H H

h h h

Happy
Horse

If you rode the horse where would you go?

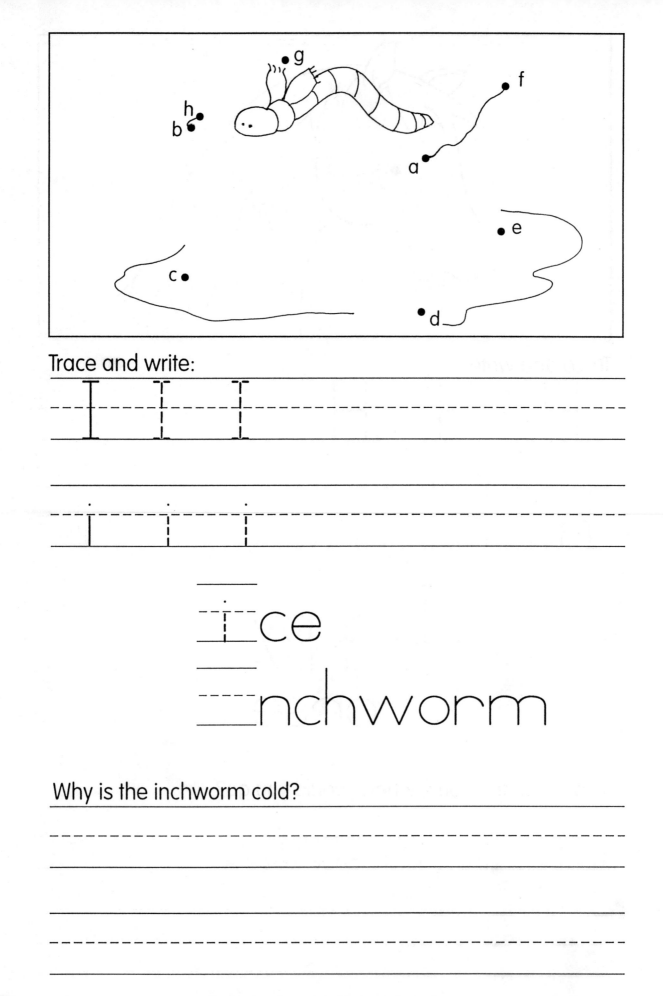

Trace and write:

I I I

i i i

Ice

Inchworm

Why is the inchworm cold?

Trace and write:

J J J

J J J

Jelly Jar

Joey

Make jelly in the jar for the baby kangaroo.
What kind did you make?

Tracing and printing letters and words

Trace and write:

K K K

k k k

Kite

Kind King

Make a kite for the king.
Tell what the kite looks like.

Trace and write:

Little
Lamb

Who is standing next to the little lamb?

Tracing and printing letters and words

Trace and write:

M M M

m m m

me _ _y

_onkey

What can the monkey do?

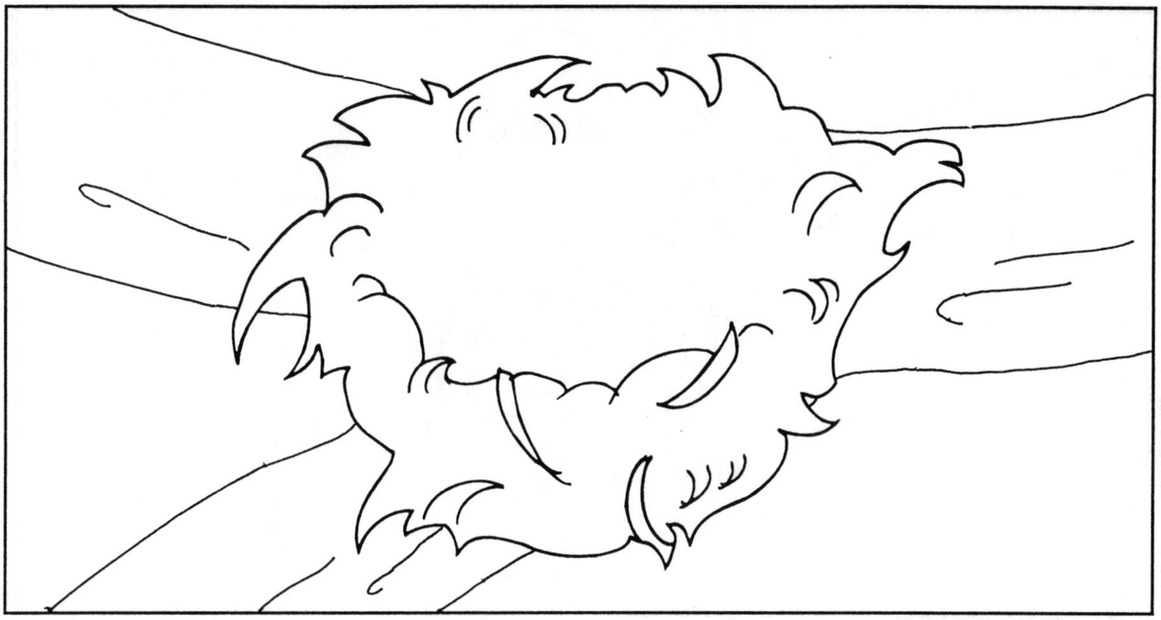

Trace and write:

N N N

n n n

nine   nuts

nest

Draw nine nuts in the nest.
Tell what you did.

Tracing and printing letters and words   **175**

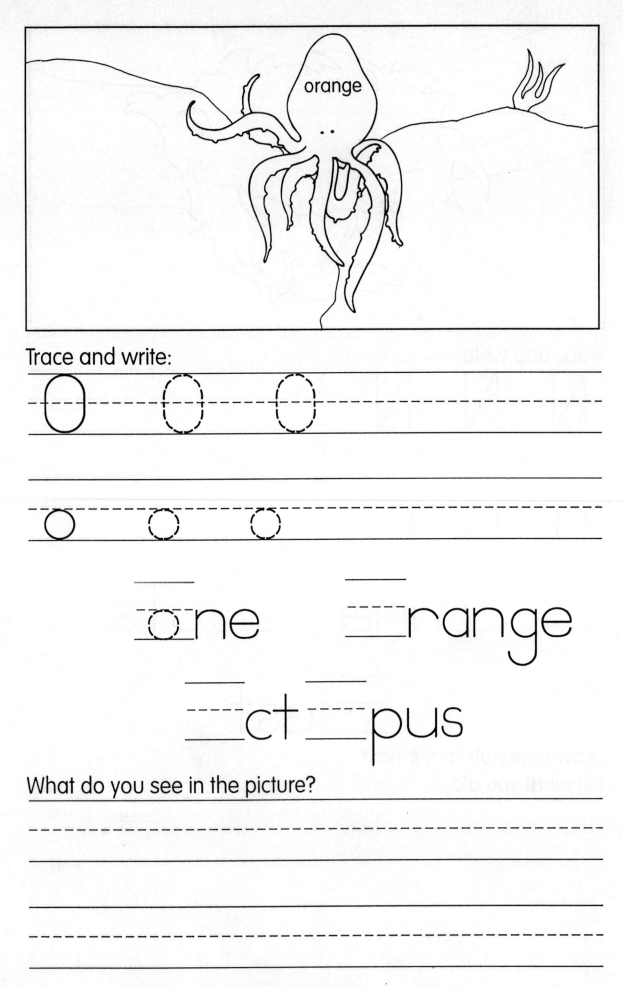

orange

Trace and write:

O   O   O

O   O   O

Ởne   Ởrange

Ởct Ởpus

What do you see in the picture?

Tracing and printing letters and words

Trace and write:

P   P   P

p   p   p

pan   et

   u   y

What do you see in the picture?

Tracing and printing letters and words   **177**

Trace and write:

Q Q Q

q q q

queen

quilt

What is the queen making?

Tracing and printing letters and words

Trace and write:

R R R

r r r

red

ose

What color is the rose?

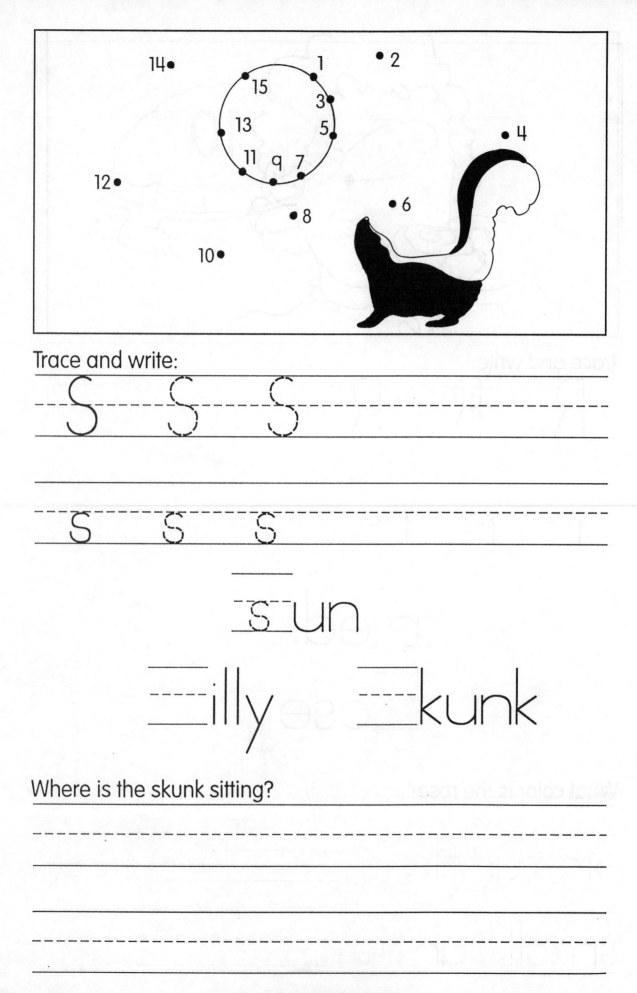

Trace and write:

S   S   S

s   s   s

sun

silly   skunk

Where is the skunk sitting?

Tracing and printing letters and words

Trace and write:

T ⊤ ⊤

t ⊤ ⊤

Turtle

Ten Two

What numbers are on the turtles?

big turtle _____

small turtle _____

Tracing and printing letters and words

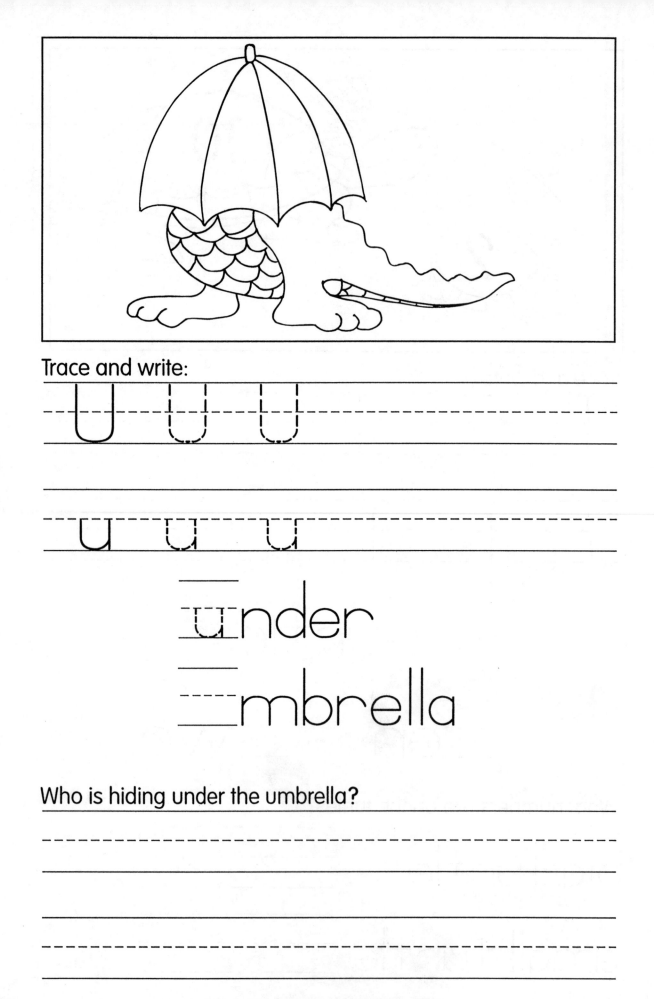

Trace and write:

U U U

u u u

under

Umbrella

Who is hiding under the umbrella?

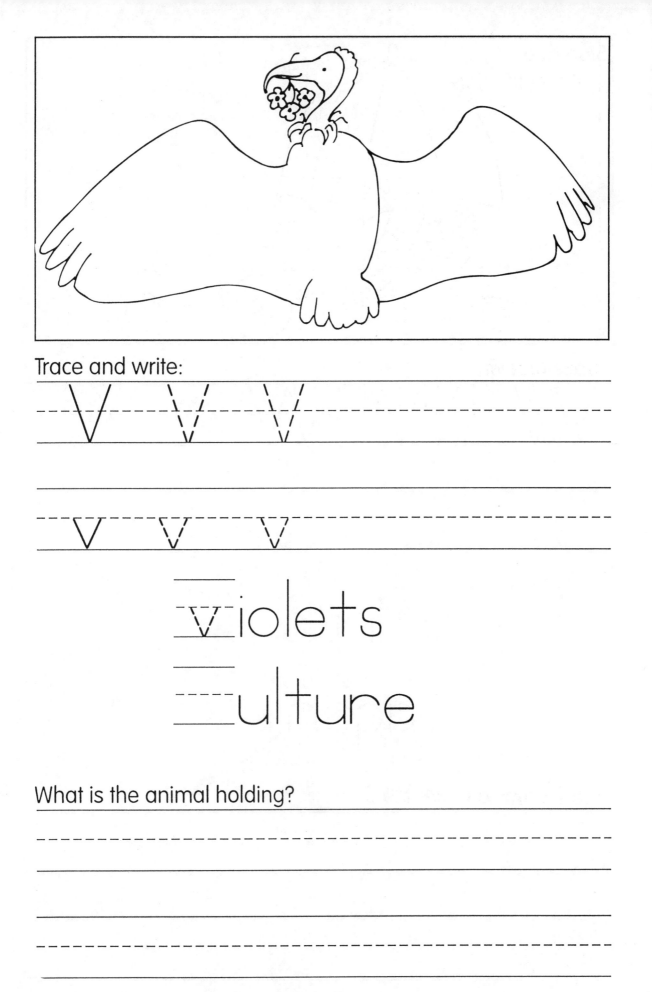

Trace and write:

V   V   V

V   V   V

Violets

Culture

What is the animal holding?

Start at **a**.
Connect the dots.

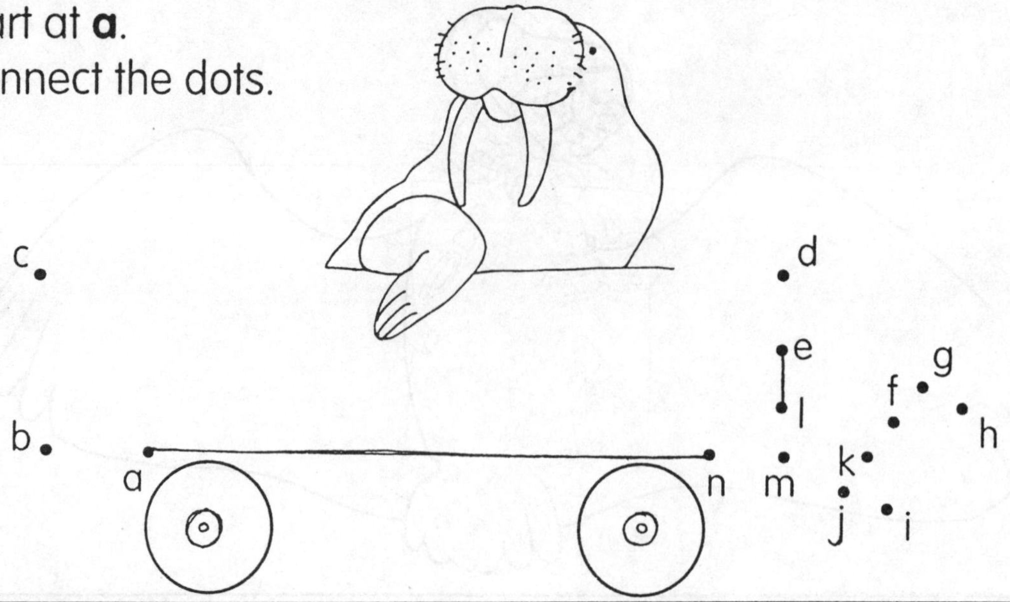

c•

•d

•e
•l

•g
•f
•h

b•
a

n m •k
j •i

Trace and write:

W W W

W W W

walrus

agon

Where is the walrus?

Trace and write:

X   X   X

X   X   X

X-ray

fo__ in so__

What is the fox getting?

Tracing and printing letters and words

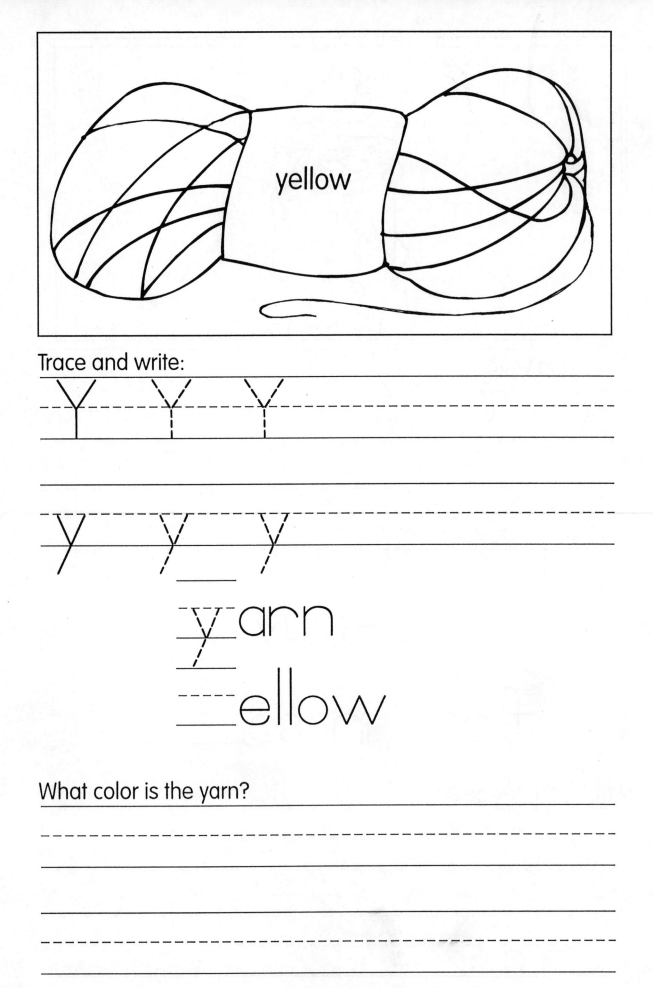

yellow

Trace and write:

Y   Y   Y

y   y   y

yarn

yellow

What color is the yarn?

Tracing and printing letters and words

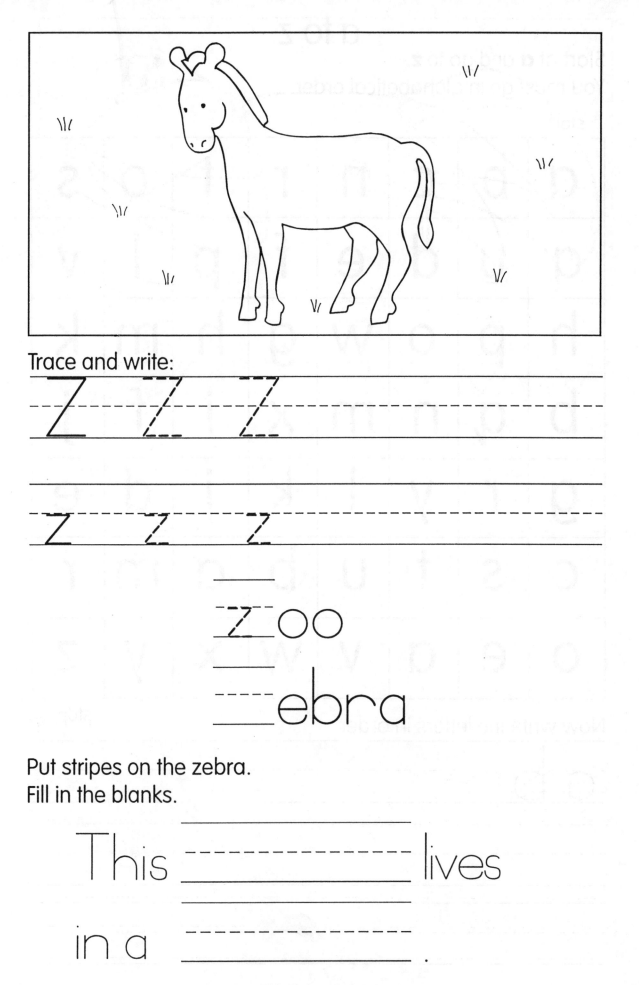

Trace and write:

Z Z Z Z

z z z z

z oo

z ebra

Put stripes on the zebra.
Fill in the blanks.

This _____ lives

in a _____.

a to z

Start at **a** and go to **z**.
You must go in alphabetical order.

start

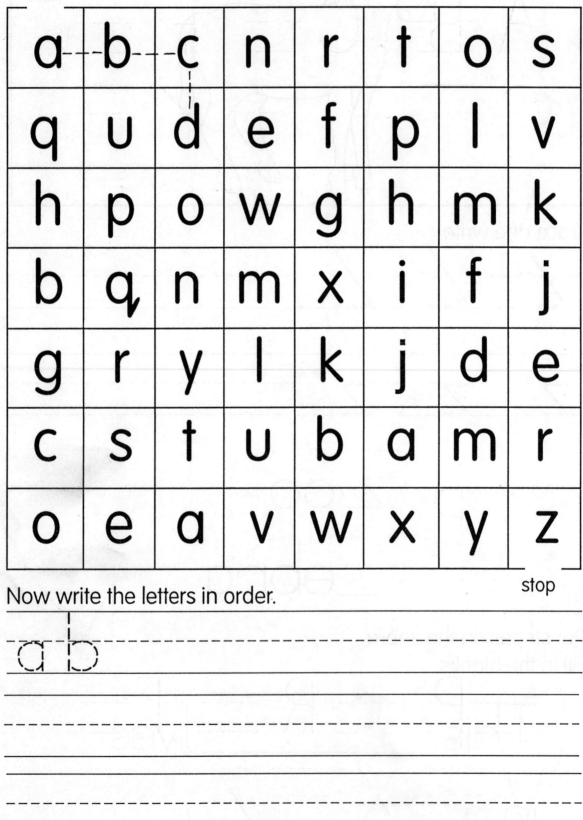

a	b	c	n	r	t	o	s
q	u	d	e	f	p	l	v
h	p	o	w	g	h	m	k
b	q	n	m	x	i	f	j
g	r	y	l	k	j	d	e
c	s	t	u	b	a	m	r
o	e	a	v	w	x	y	z

stop

Now write the letters in order.

a b

Understanding alphabetic order; printing

Fill in the Missing Letters

Understanding alphabetic order; printing   **189**

My Name

first

middle

last

Draw yourself here.

Printing my name

Where I Live

Here is my address.

number and street

town

state

zip code

This is where I live.

Copy this Poem

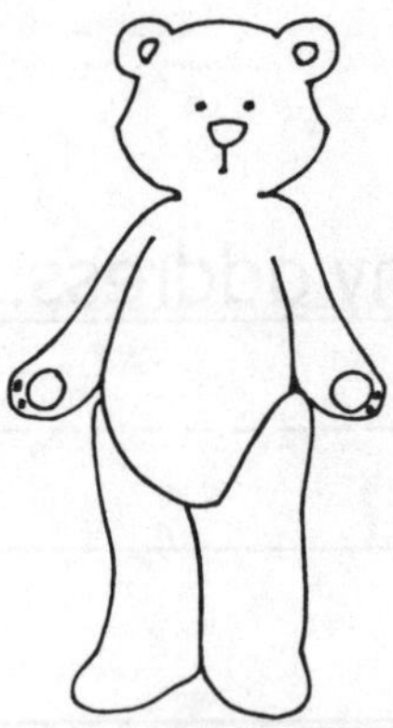

Fuzzy Wuzzy was a bear.

Fuzzy Wuzzy had no hair.

Fuzzy wasn't very fuzzy.

Was he?

Printing a poem

Bb

bat

What starts with **b**?

Recognizing initial consonant sounds

Rr　　rabbit

What starts with **r** ?

Ff

fox

What starts with **f**?

Recognizing initial consonant sounds

195

Kk

<u>k</u>ite

What starts with **<u>k</u>** ?

Recognizing initial consonant sounds

Match:

k

b

f

r

Beginning Sounds

b f r k

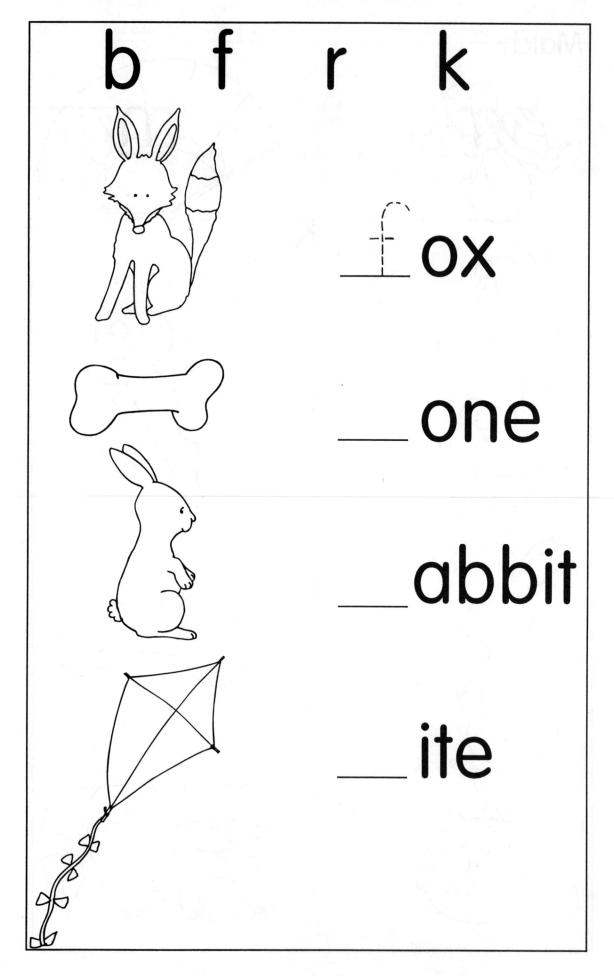

__f__ox

__one

__abbit

__ite

Recognizing initial consonant sounds and printing the letters

Mm

man

What starts with **m** ?

Recognizing initial consonant sounds

Ss   sun

What starts with **s** ?

Recognizing initial consonant sounds

Gg

goat

What starts with **g**_?

Hh

hen

What starts with **h** ?

Recognizing initial consonant sounds

Match:

6

m

s

g

h

Beginning Sounds

m s g h

_m_ouse

__ ock

__ oat

__ en

Recognizing initial consonant sounds and printing the letters

Jj

jar

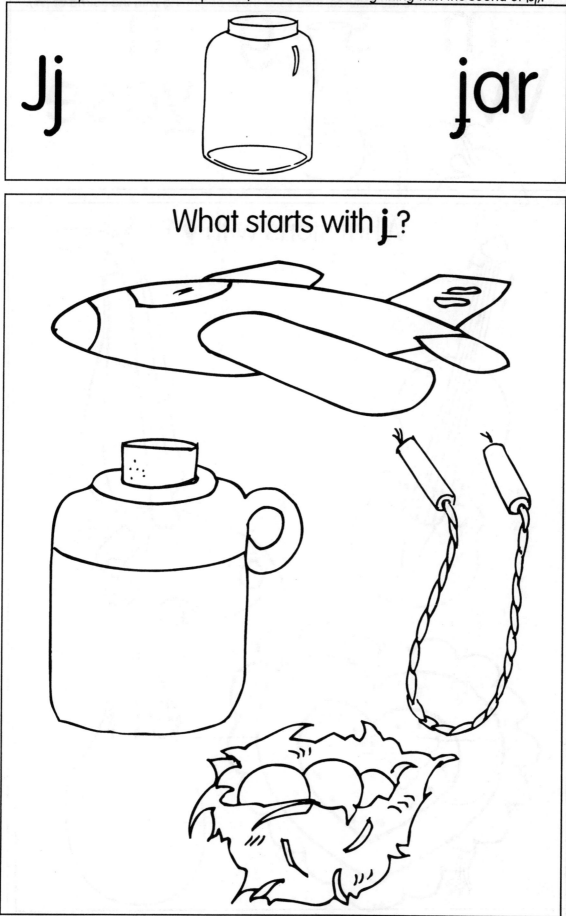

What starts with j_?

Recognizing initial consonant sounds

Vv

vase

What starts with v ?

Recognizing initial consonant sounds

Ll

<u>l</u>og

What starts with <u>l</u>?

Beginning Sounds

Recognizing initial consonant sounds

207

Note: Have your child name the pictures, then color those beginning with the sound of (Dd).

Dd

<u>d</u>uck

What starts with <u>**d**</u> ?

208

Recognizing initial consonant sounds

Match:

j

v

l

d

Recognizing initial consonant sounds

j v l d

__j__ar

___og

___uck

___ase

Recognizing initial consonant sounds and printing the letters

Nn   9   <u>n</u>ine

What starts with **<u>n</u>** ?

Recognizing initial consonant sounds

Pp

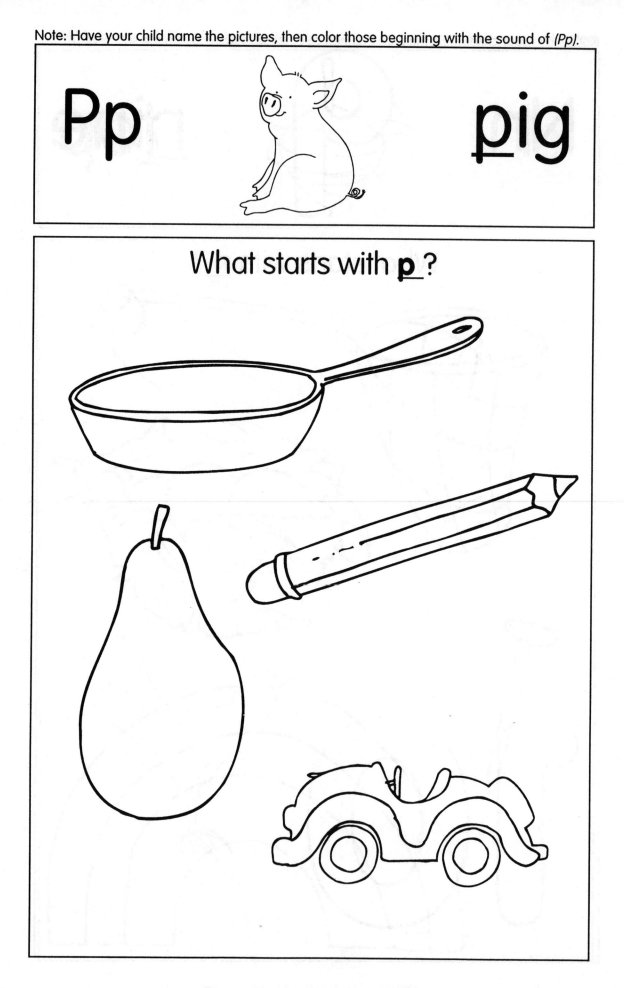

pig

What starts with **p**_?

Recognizing initial consonant sounds

Note: Have your child name the pictures, then color those beginning with the sound of *(Tt)*.

Tt

top

What starts with **t** ?

Recognizing initial consonant sounds

Zz  zipper

What starts with z ?

Recognizing initial consonant sounds

Match:

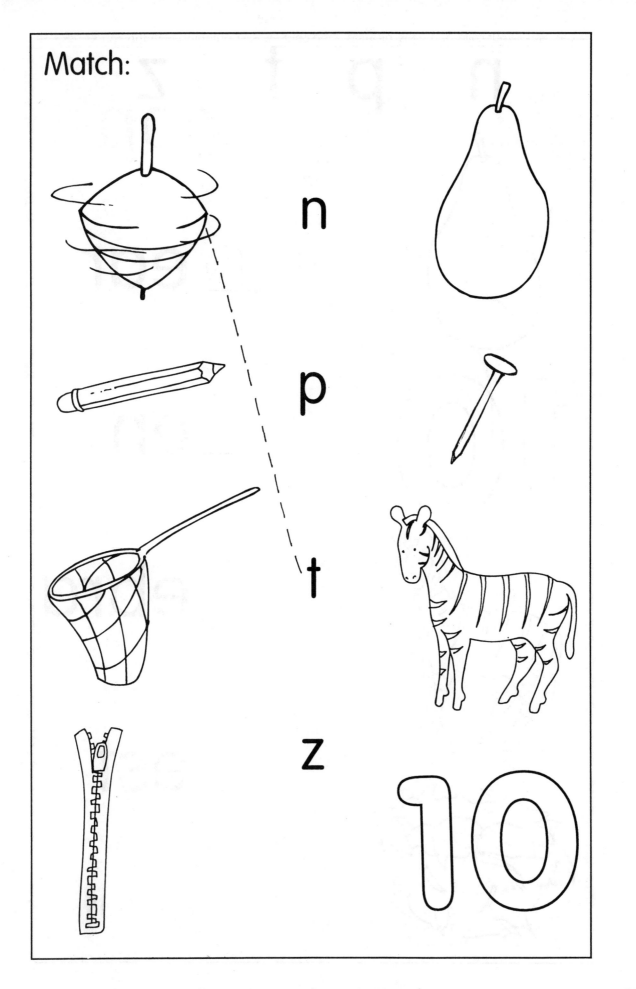

n

p

t

z

Recognizing initial consonant sounds

n p t z

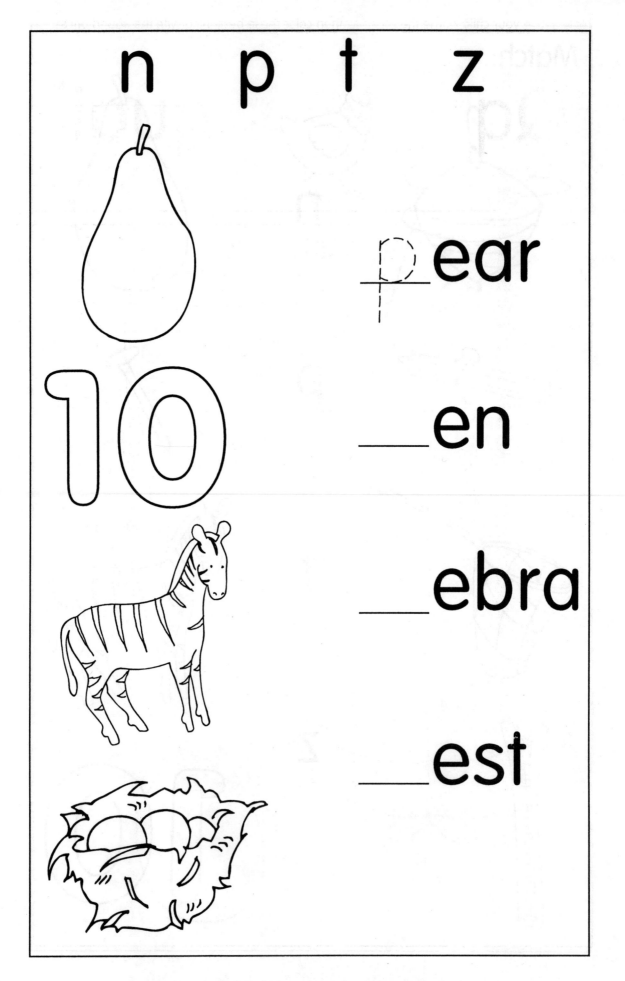

p ear

___ en

___ ebra

___ est

Recognizing initial consonant sounds and printing the letters

Qq  quail

What starts with q?

Beginning Sounds

Ww web

What starts with **w**?

Recognizing initial consonant sounds

Yy   yo   yo

What starts with **y**_?

Recognizing initial consonant sounds   **219**

Cc

cake

What starts with **c** ?

q w y c

__q__uail

___arn

___ake

___agon

Beginning Sounds

Answer Key

Please take time to go over the work your child has completed. Ask your child to explain what he/she has done. Praise both success and effort. If mistakes have been made, explain what the answer should have been and how to find it. Let your child know that mistakes are a part of learning. The time you spend with your child helps let him/her know you feel learning is important.

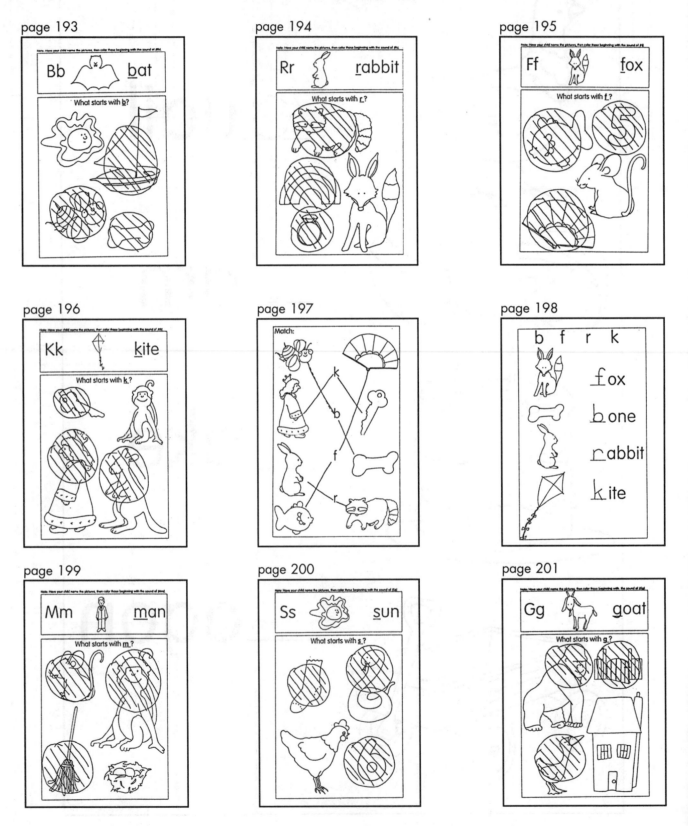

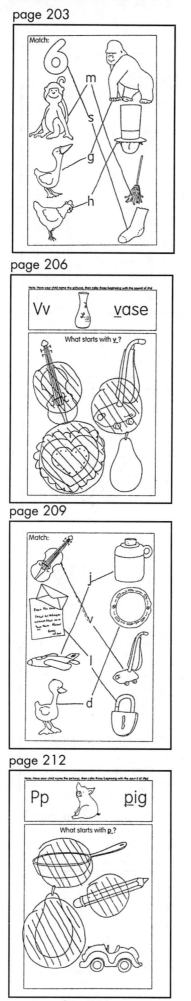

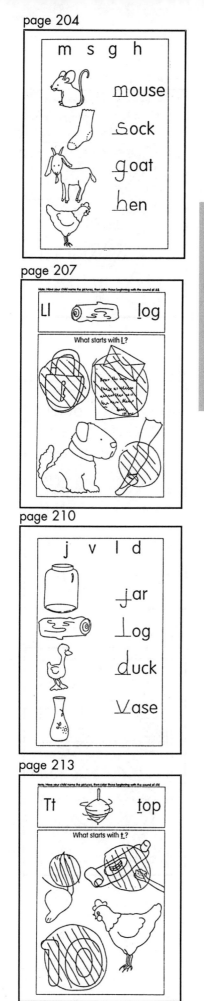

Answers

page 214

Note: Have your child name the pictures, then color those beginning with the sound of /z/.

Zz 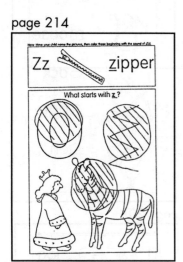 **zipper**

What starts with **z**?

page 215

Match:

n

p

t

z

10

page 216

n p t z

10

p̶ear

t̶en

z̶ebra

n̶est

page 217

Note: Have your child name the pictures, then color those beginning with the sound of /kw/.

Qq  **quail**

What starts with **q**?

page 218

Note: Have your child name the pictures, then color those beginning with the sound of /w/.

Ww **web**

What starts with **w**?

page 219

Note: Have your child name the pictures, then color those beginning with the sound of /y/.

Yy  **yo yo**

What starts with **y**?

page 220

Note: Have your child name the pictures, then color those beginning with the sound of /c/.

Cc **cake**

What starts with **c**?

page 221

q w y c

quail

yarn

cake

wagon

Note: Have the child name the pictures, listening to the sound of the letter **a**, then complete the page.

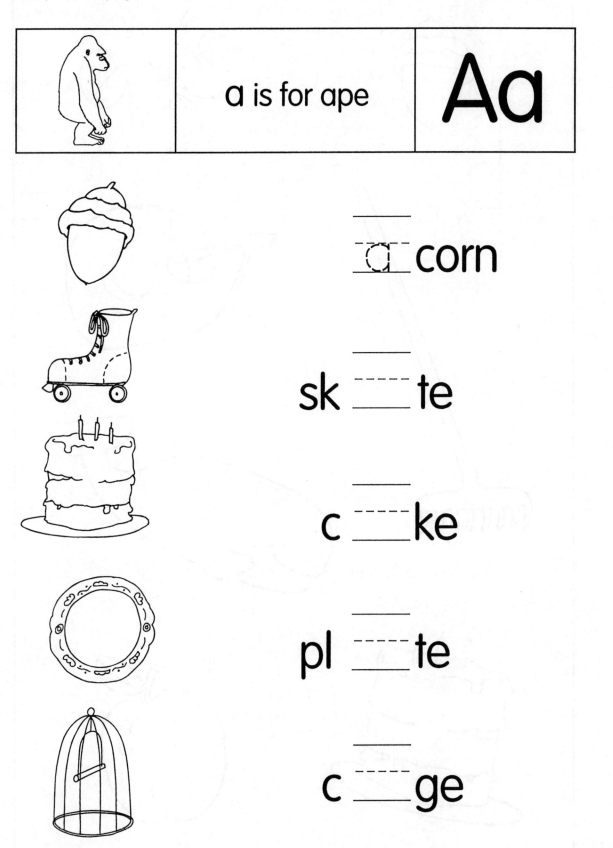

a is for ape

Aa

___ a corn

sk ___ te

c ___ ke

pl ___ te

c ___ ge

Recognizing a long vowel sound and printing the letter

Circle long <u>a</u>   X short <u>a</u>

Recognizing a long vowel sound

Start at 1.
Connect the dots.

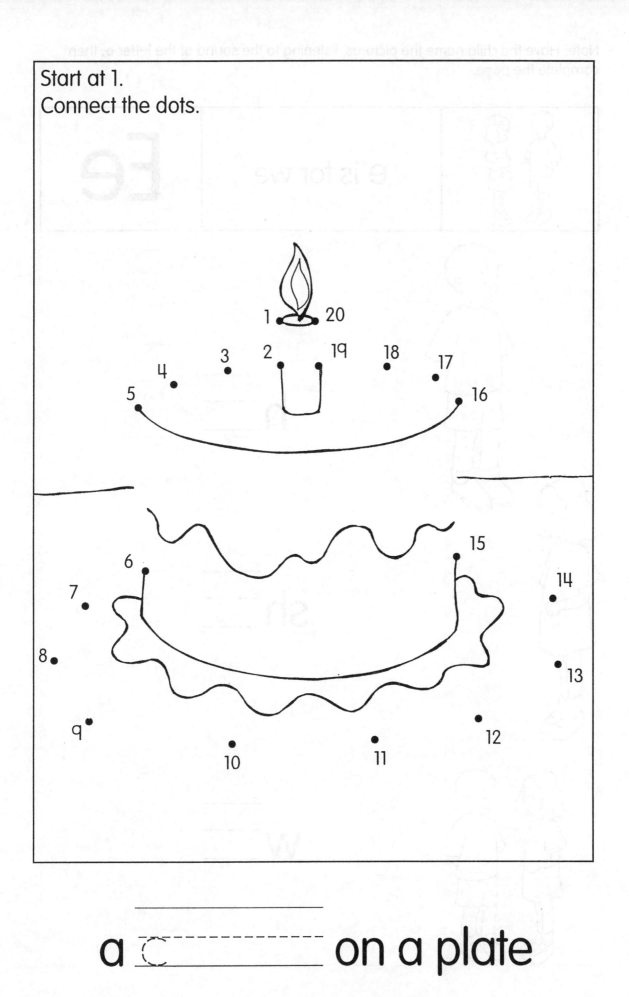

a c_____ on a plate

Note: Have the child name the pictures, listening to the sound of the letter **e**, then complete the page.

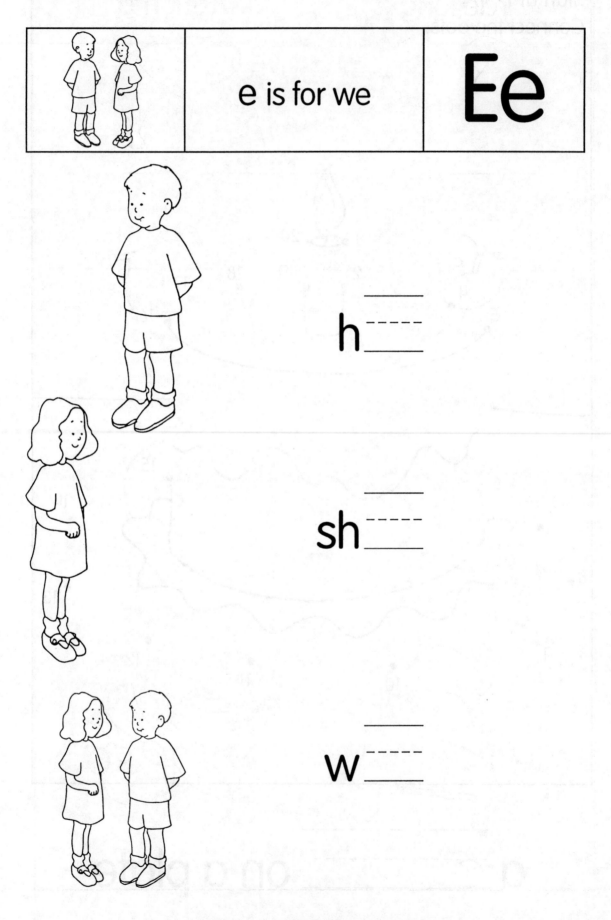

e is for we

Ee

h_____

sh_____

w_____

Recognizing a long vowel sound and printing the letter

Circle long e   X short e

Long Vowels

Note: Have the child name the pictures, listening to the sound of the letter **i**, then complete the page.

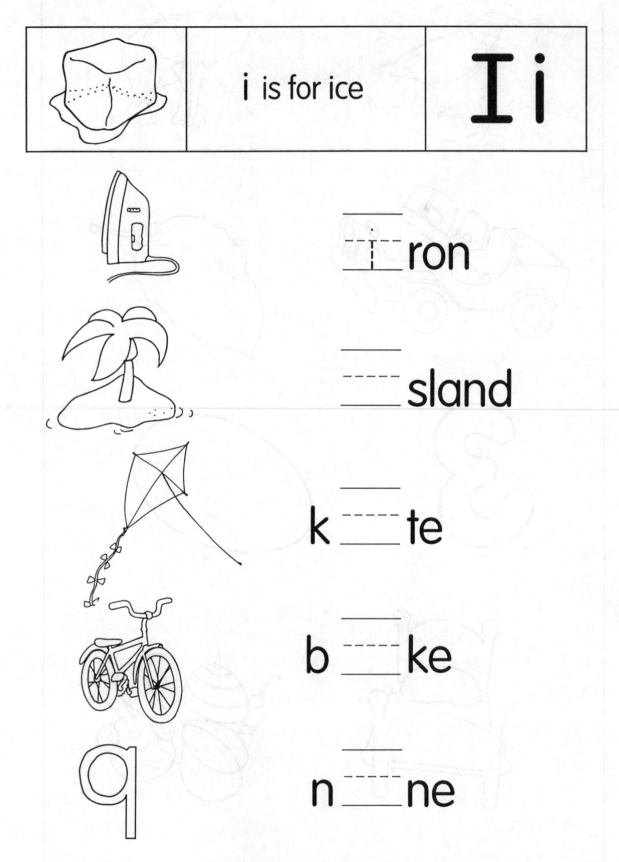

i is for ice

I i

‾‾ı‾‾ron

‾‾‾‾‾sland

k ‾‾‾‾ te

b ‾‾‾‾ ke

n ‾‾‾‾ ne

Recognizing a long vowel sound and printing the letter

Circle long i   X short i

Recognizing a long vowel sound

Start at 1.
Connect the dots.

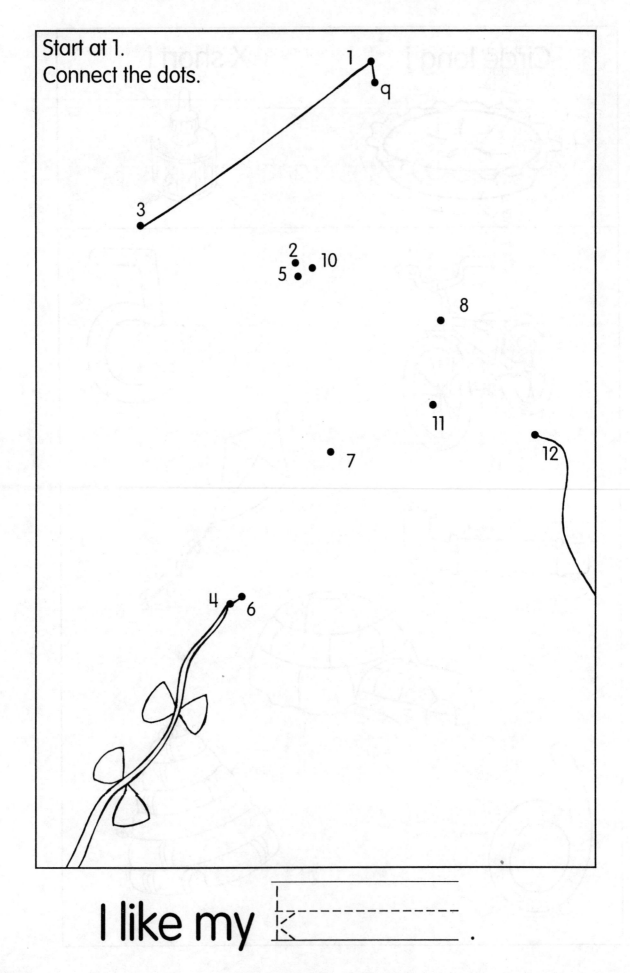

I like my _____ .

Printing a long vowel word

Note: Have the child name the pictures, listening to the sound of the letter **o**, then complete the page.

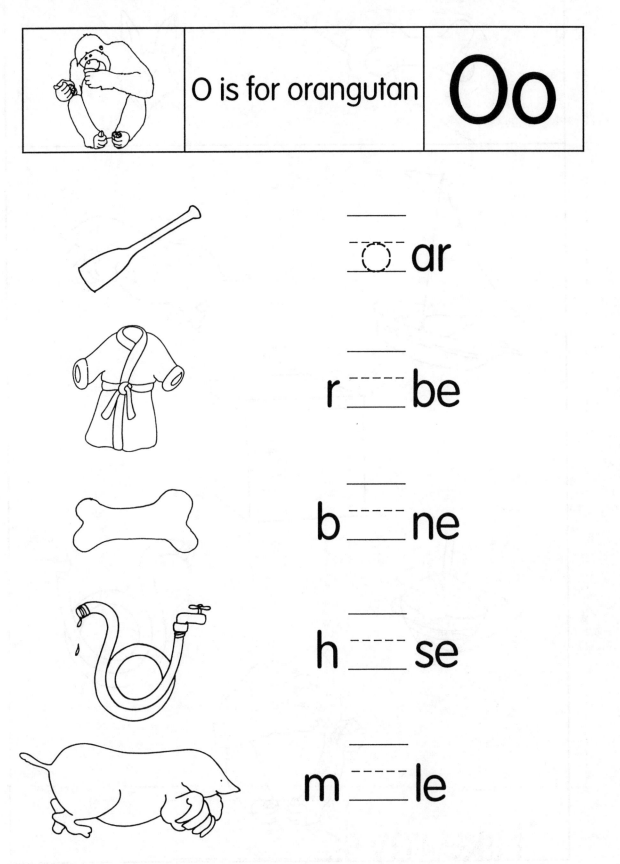

O is for orangutan   Oo

o̅ ar

r o̅ be

b o̅ ne

h o̅ se

m o̅ le

Circle long <u>o</u>   X short <u>o</u>

Recognizing a long vowel sound

Note: Have the child name the pictures, listening to the sound of the letter **u**, then complete the page.

u is for unicorn

Uu

m __u__ le

t ___ be

c ___ be

___ kelele

m ___ sic

Long Vowels

Circle long <u>u</u>   X short <u>u</u>

Recognizing a long vowel word

Match the vowel sounds.

Note: Explain to your learner what usually happens when you add a **silent e** to a short vowel word. The vowel becomes a long sound.

Silent e

Read.	Add an <u>e</u> and read.	
can	can<u>e</u> ___	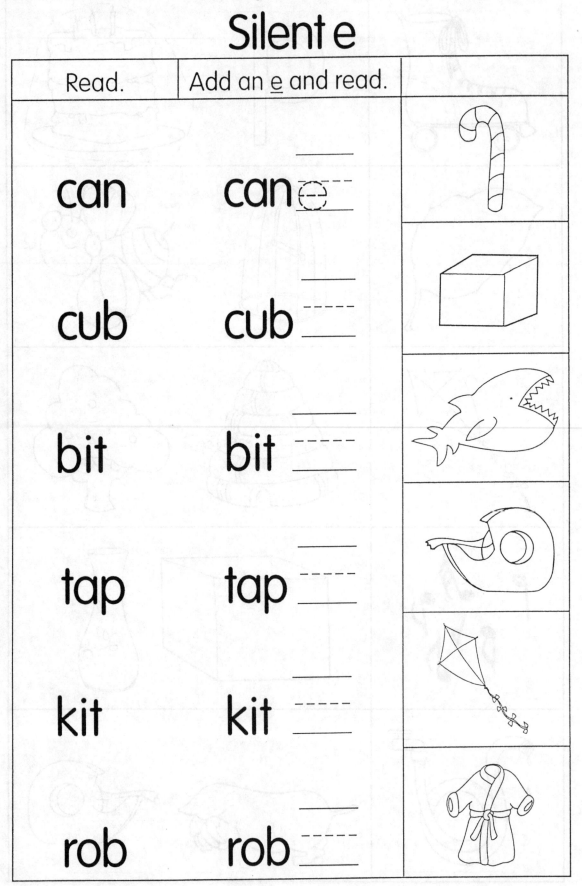
cub	cub ___	
bit	bit ___	
tap	tap ___	
kit	kit ___	
rob	rob ___	

Understanding silent e

Yes or No

He is in the cage.

| (yes) | no |

Five eggs are on the plate.

| yes | no |

Feed me a bone.

| yes | no |

Kate can ride the bike.

| yes | no |

Match:

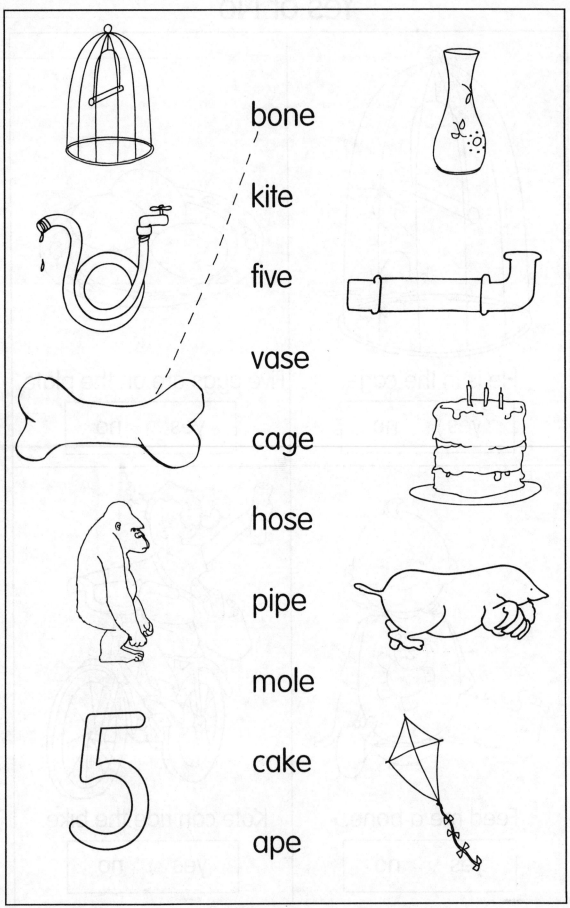

bone

kite

five

vase

cage

hose

pipe

mole

cake

ape

5

Reading to match pictures and words

Read and Draw

a name
on the line

a big cake on the
blue plate

a kite up in the tree

a snake on the
brown gate

Note: Two vowels together can make a long vowel sound.

b<u>ee</u>

tr <u>e</u> <u>e</u>

j ___ ___ p

thr ___ ___

___ ___ l

kn ___ ___

Read these words to someone.

Recognizing a long vowel sound and printing the letter

Match:

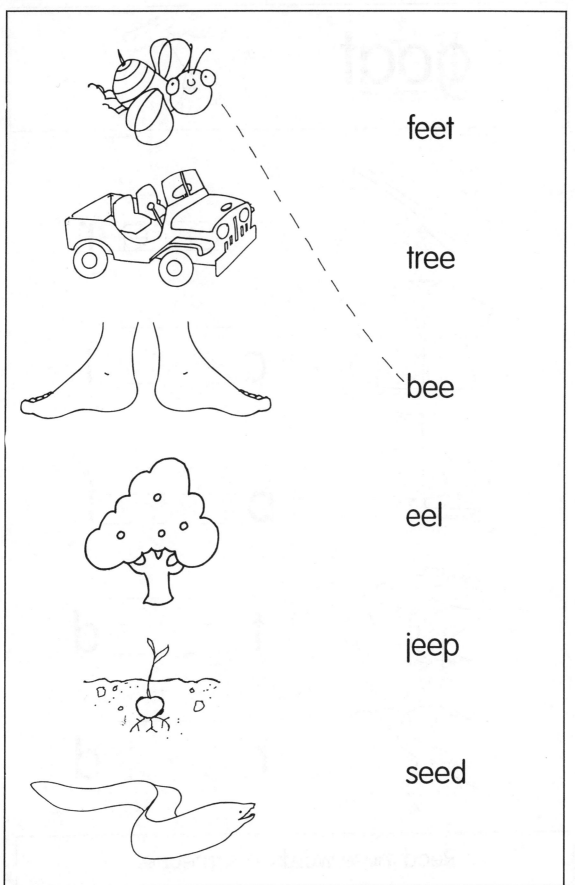

feet

tree

bee

eel

jeep

seed

Note: Two vowels together can make a long vowel sound.

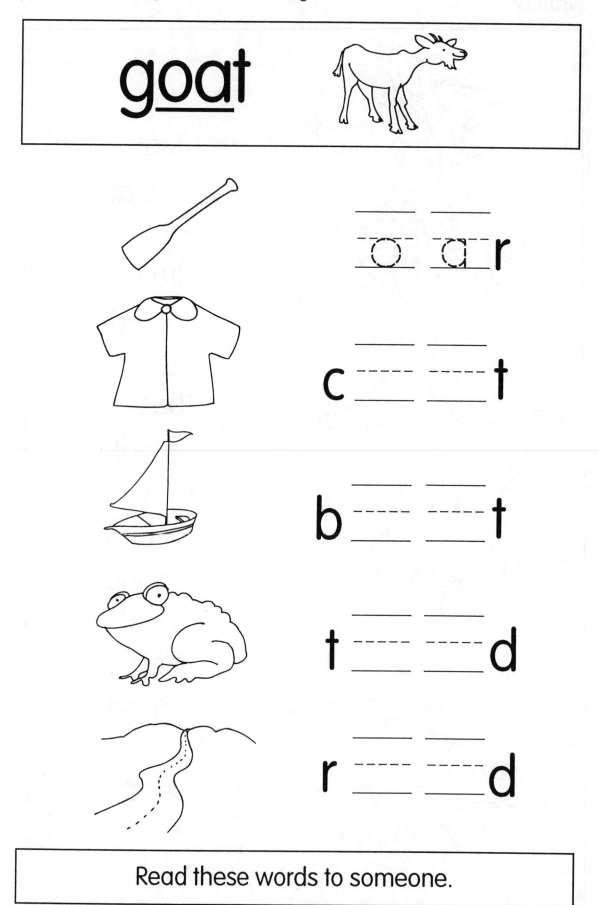

g__o__at

oar

c__ __t

b__ __t

t__ __d

r__ __d

Read these words to someone.

Recognizing a long vowel sound and printing the letters

Match:

goat

toad

coat

soap

road

Note: Two vowels together can make a long vowel sound.

p<u>ai</u>l

sn __a__ __i__ l

qu __ __ l

p __ __ nt

r __ __ n

tr __ __ n

Read these words to someone.

Recognizing a long vowel sound and printing the letters

Match:

paint

rain

quail

pail

mail

train

Color the Puzzle

blue	yellow	red
<u>ai</u>	<u>oa</u>	<u>ee</u>

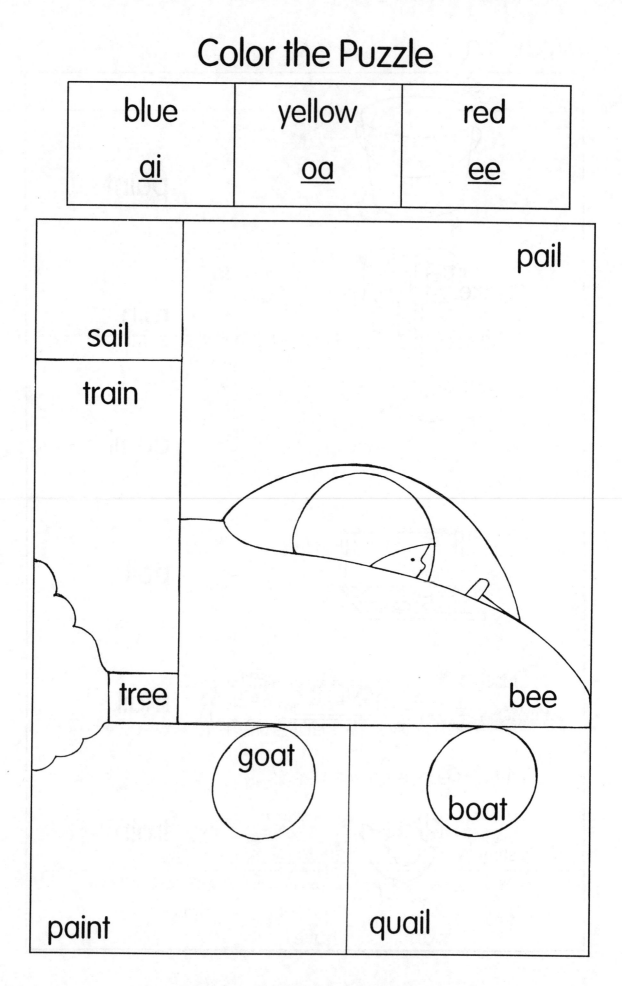

pail

sail

train

tree

bee

goat

boat

paint

quail

Recognizing long vowel sounds; following directions

Pets at School

"Wake up, Eve," said June.

"Miss Lane said we can take pets to school.

I don't want to be late."

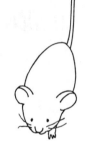

"This is my pet cat," said June.

"His name is Dave.

He likes to take naps on my bed."

"I have three pet mice," said Zeke.

"My mom and dad gave them to me.

My mice like to eat seeds."

I read this story to _____.

Note: You may need to help your learner with the special words below.
said   school   this
want   have

"This is my dog, Mike," said Kate.
"Sit, Mike. Shake my hand.
He wants a bone to eat."

"I have a pet," said Miss Lane.
It is long and has scales.
"It is a black snake!"

We had fun with the pets at school.

I read this story to _____.

Read the story again.
Circle the long vowel words.

("Wake)(up,)(Eve,)"

Reading; recognizing long vowel words

Fill in the blanks.

Zeke has pet   mice

Miss Lane has a pet   _____

June has a pet   _____

Kate has a pet   _____

Draw your pet here.

My pet's name is   _____

The Birthday Party

My birthday is on June 16.
I sent a note to my friends.
The note said,

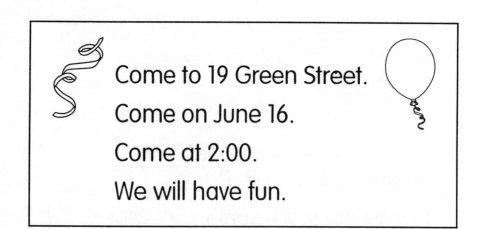

Come to 19 Green Street.
Come on June 16.
Come at 2:00.
We will have fun.

Note: You may need to help your learner with the special words below.

birthday   have   party   my
friends   said   play

My dad will bake a big cake.

He will make it look like a kite.

Mom will make hot dogs and get grape pop.

We will play games.

I read this story to _____.

Read the story again.
Put a line under long vowel words.

Dad will bake a cake.

Answer Key

Please take time to go over the work your child has completed. Ask your child to explain what he/she has done. Praise both success and effort. If mistakes have been made, explain what the answer should have been and how to find it. Let your child know that mistakes are a part of learning. The time you spend with your child helps let him/her know you feel learning is important.

page 225
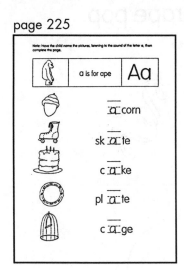

page 226
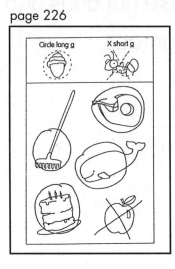

page 227
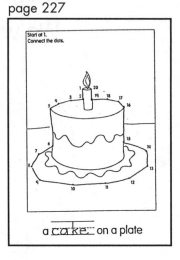

page 228

page 229
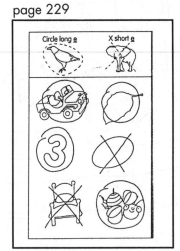

page 230
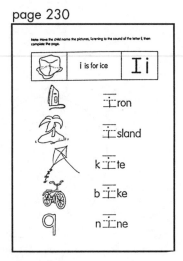

page 231
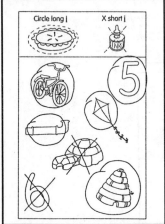

page 232
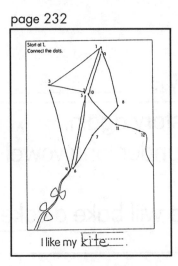

page 233

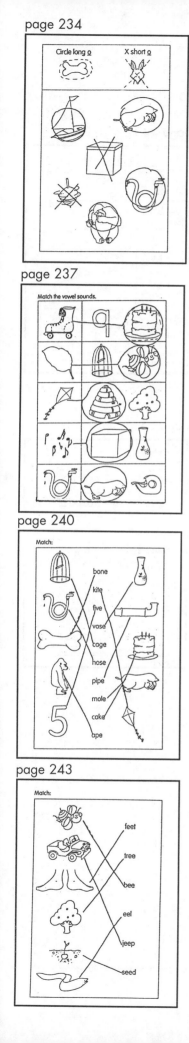

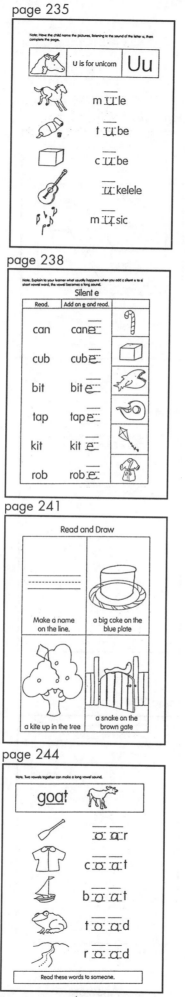

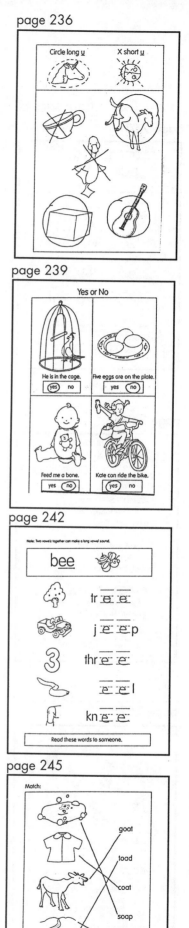

page 234

Circle long o   X short o

page 235

Note: Have the child name the pictures, listening to the sound of the letter u, then complete the page.

u is for unicorn   Uu

m u le
t u be
c u be
u kelele
m u sic

page 236

Circle long u   X short u

page 237

Match the vowel sounds.

page 238

Note: Explain to your learner what usually happens when you add a silent e to a short vowel word, the vowel becomes a long sound.

Silent e

Read.	Add an e and read.	
can	can e	
cub	cub e	
bit	bit e	
tap	tap e	
kit	kit e	
rob	rob e	

page 239

Yes or No

He is in the cage. — yes **no**
Five eggs are on the plate. — yes **no**
Feed me a bone. — yes **no**
Kate can ride the bike. — **yes** no

page 240

Match:

bone
kite
five
vase
cage
hose
pipe
mole
cake
ape

page 241

Read and Draw

Make a name on the line.
a big cake on the blue plate
a kite up in the tree
a snake on the brown gate

page 242

Note: Two vowels together can make a long vowel sound.

bee

tr ee
j ee p
thr ee
ee l
kn ee

Read these words to someone.

page 243

Match:

feet
tree
bee
eel
jeep
seed

page 244

Note: Two vowels together can make a long vowel sound.

goat

o a r
c oa t
b oa t
t oa d
r oa d

Read these words to someone.

page 245

Match:

goat
toad
coat
soap
road

Answers

255

page 246

Note: Two vowels together can make a long vowel sound.

pail

sn**ai**l

qu**ai**l

p**ai**nt

r**ai**n

tr**ai**n

Read these words to someone.

page 247

Match:

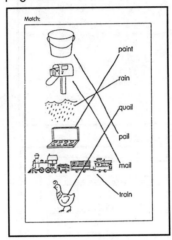

paint
rain
quail
pail
mail
train

page 248

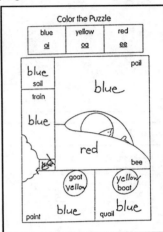

Color the Puzzle

blue	yellow	red
ai	oa	ee

pail
blue
sail
train
blue
blue
red
bee
goat yellow
yellow boat
paint
blue
quail
blue
bee

page 249

Pets at School

"Wake up, Eve," said June.

"Miss Lane said we can take pets to school."

"I don't want to be late."

"This is my pet cat," said June.

"His name is Dave."

"He likes to take naps on my bed."

"I have three pet mice," said Zeke.

"My mom and dad gave them to me."

"My mice like to eat seeds."

I read this story to _____

Note: You may need to help your learner with the special words below.
said   school   this
want   have

page 250

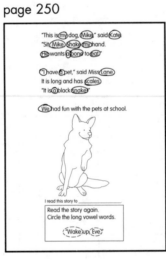

"This is my dog, Mike," said Kate.
"Sit, Mike. Shake my hand.
He wants a bone to eat."

"I have a pet," said Miss Lane.
It is long and has scales.
"It is a black snake."

We had fun with the pets at school.

I read this story to _____

Read the story again.
Circle the long vowel words.

Wake up, Eve.

page 251

Fill in the blanks.

Zeke has pet   mice

Miss Lane has a pet   snake

June has a pet   cat

Kate has a pet   dog

Draw your pet here.

will vary

My pet's name is _____

page 252

The Birthday Party

My birthday is on June 16.
I sent a note to my friends.
The note said,

Come to 19 Green Street.
Come on June 16.
Come at 2:00.
We will have fun.

Note: You may need to help your learner with the special words below.
birthday   have   party   my
friends   said   play

page 253

My dad will bake a big cake.
He will make it look like a kite.
Mom will make hot dogs and get grape pop.
We will play games.

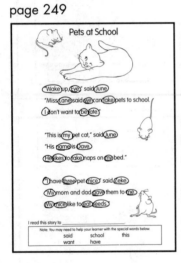

I read this story to _____

Read the story again.
Put a line under long vowel words.

Dad will bake a cake.

Note: Have the child name the pictures, listening to the short sound of the letter **a**, then complete the page.

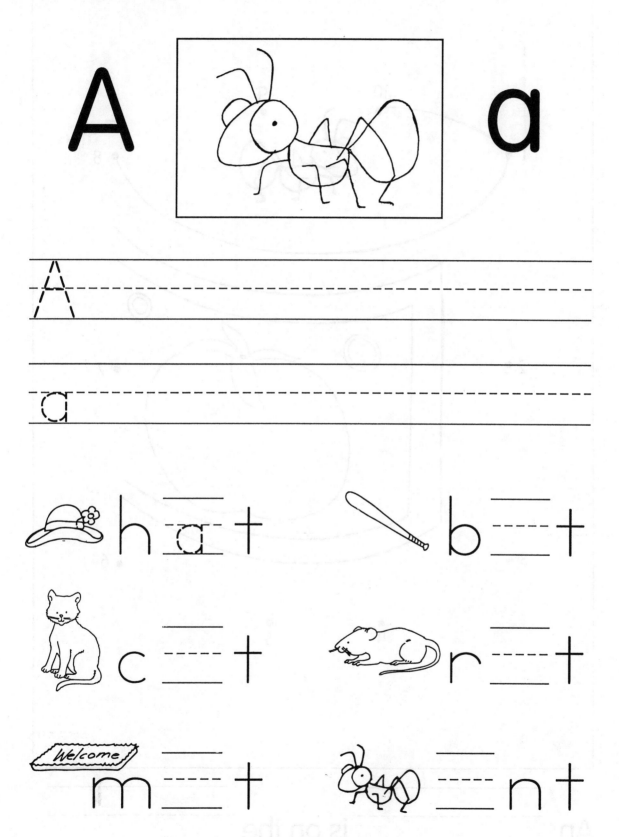

Start at 1.
Connect the dots.

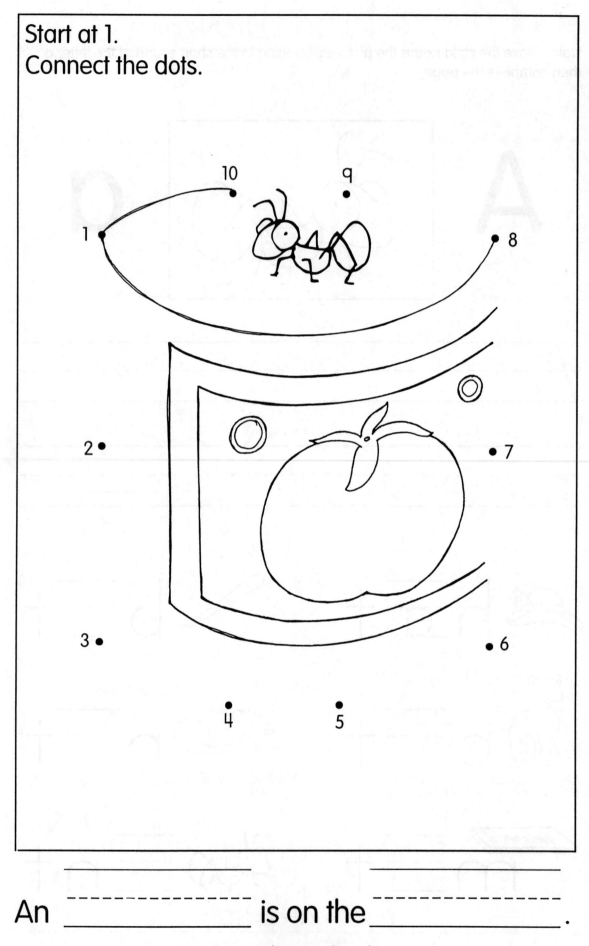

An _____ is on the _____.

Printing short vowel words

Read and Draw

a fat cat sat on a mat

a rat had a hat

Note: Have the child name the pictures, listening to the short sound of the letter **e**, then complete the page.

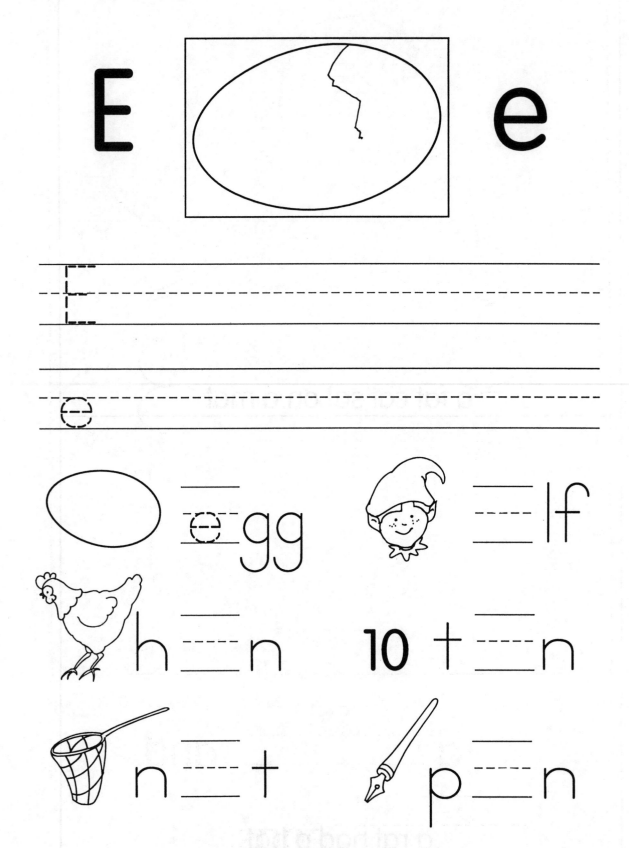

Recognizing a short vowel sound and printing the letter

Start at 1.
Connect the dots.

a _____ and

_____ eggs

Printing short vowel words

Read and Draw

an egg in a pan

a hen in a pen

Reading

Note: Have the child name the pictures, listening to the short sound of the letter **i**, then complete the page.

I

i

I - - - - - - - - - - - - - - - -

i - - - - - - - - - - - - - - - -

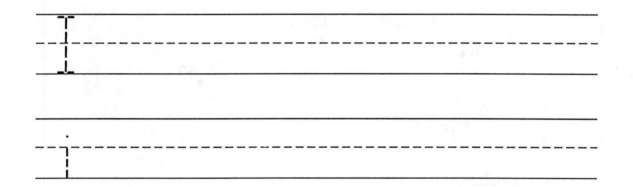

w i g   insects

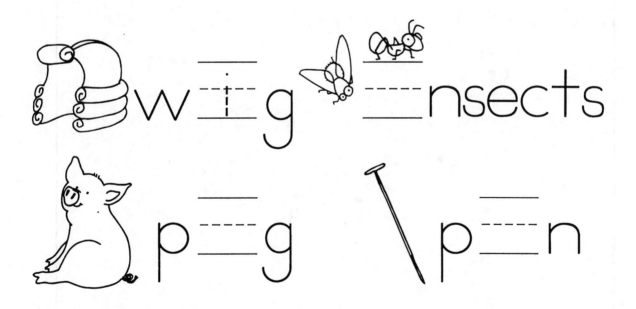

p i g   p i n

inchworm

Short Vowels

Start at 1.
Connect the dots.

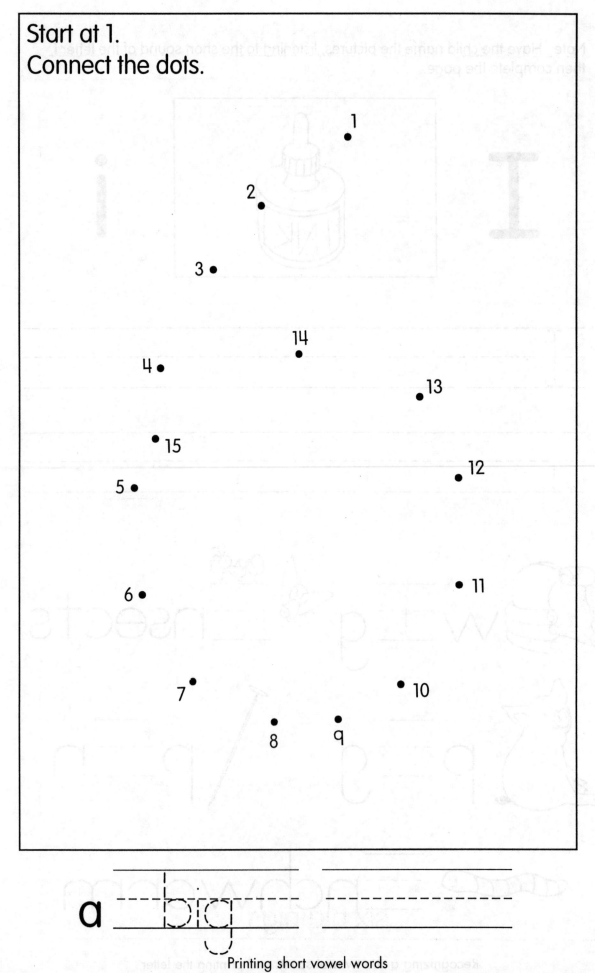

a   big

Printing short vowel words

Read and Draw

a pig in a wig

six big pigs

Note: Have the child name the pictures, listening to the short sound of the letter **o**, then complete the page.

O   o

O

o

o x   b _ x

d _ g   t _ p

_ _ tter   f _ x

Recognizing a short vowel sound and printing the letter

Start at 1.
Connect the dots.

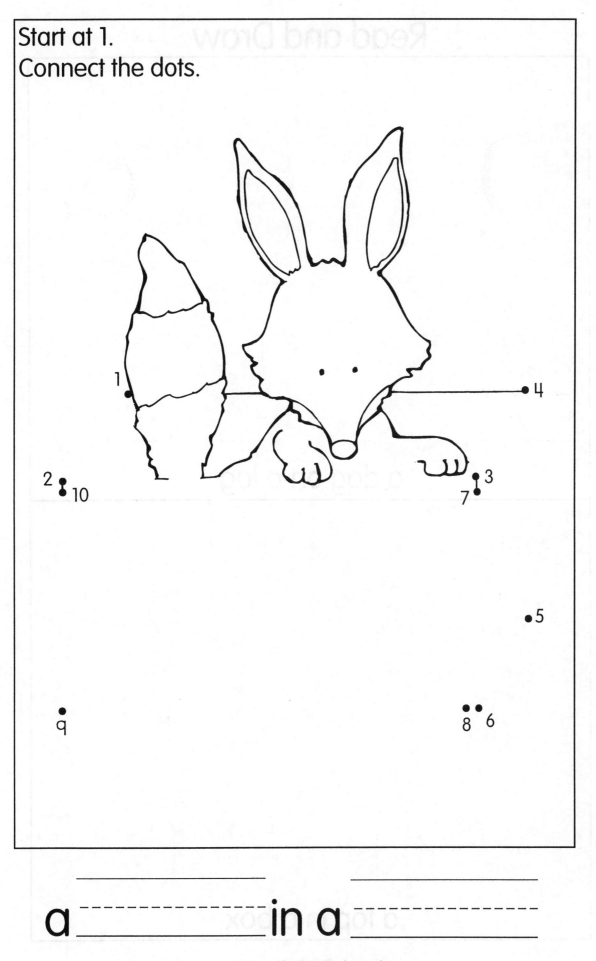

a _____ in a _____

Printing short vowel words

Read and Draw

a dog on a log

a top in a box

Note: Have the child name the pictures, listening to the short sound of the letter **u**, then complete the page.

U   u

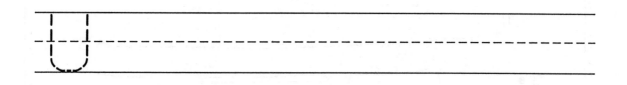

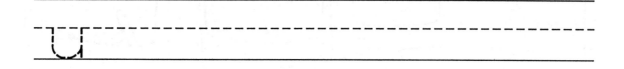

 s u n    b __ g

 b __ s   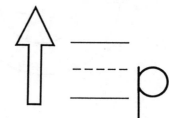 __ p

 __ mbrella

Recognizing a short vowel sound and printing the letter

Short Vowels

Start at 1.
Connect the dots.

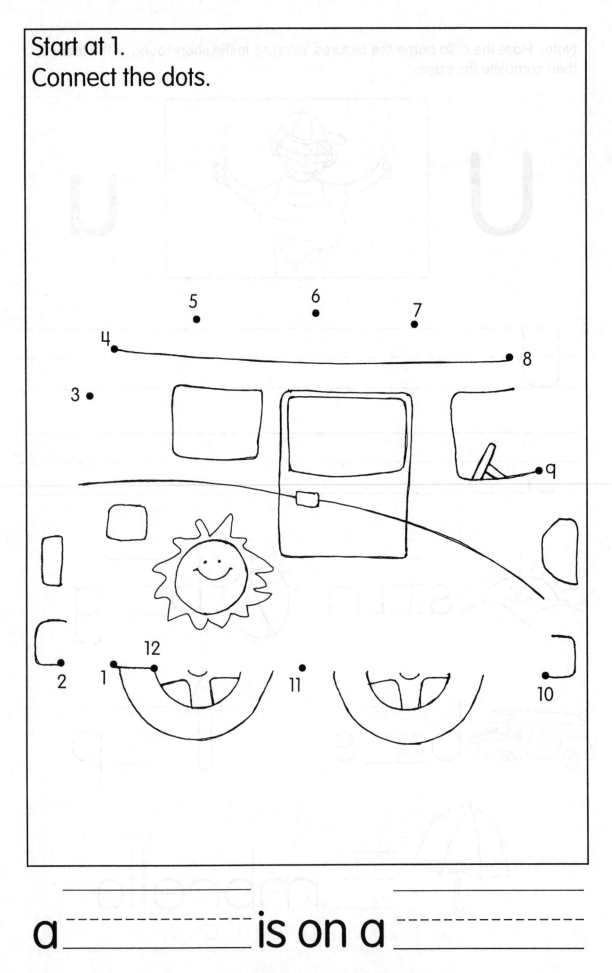

a _____ is on a _____

Printing short vowel words

Read and Draw

a nut is in a cup

a pup is in the mud

Match the vowel sounds.

Recognizing short vowel sounds

Read.
Match.

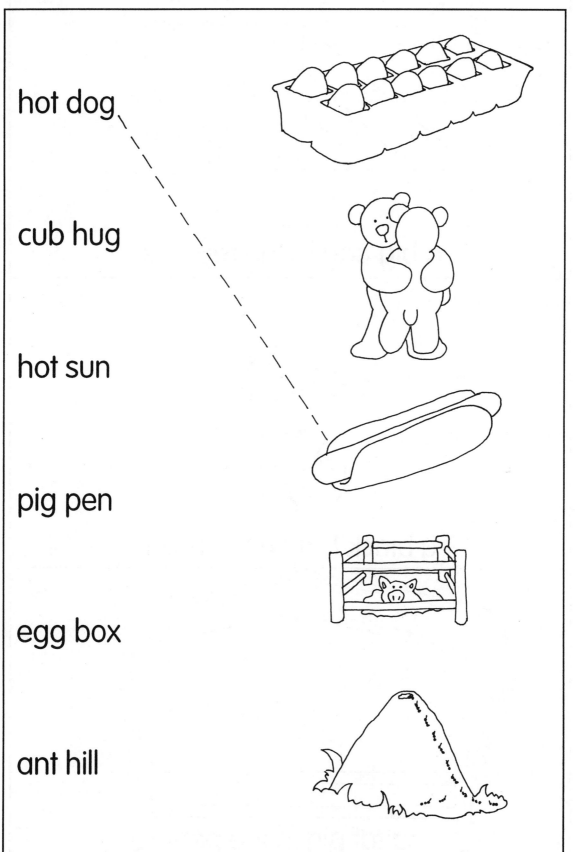

hot dog

cub hug

hot sun

pig pen

egg box

ant hill

Read and Draw

a big egg in the red box

a black hat on the man

a fat pig in the pen

Reading to follow directions

Follow the words that rhyme with <u>cat</u> to get to the <u>rat</u>.

cub	pot	cat	ten
bat	sat	hat	cot
fat	let	can	hot
mat	pat	rat	cut

Reading short vowel words

Short Vowels

Read.
Match.

a rat on a hill

an egg in a pan

a hat on a man

a dog on a log

a bat in a net

a dog in a bed

Reading to match pictures and words

Read.
Match.

The cat is fat.

The dog can run.

The fox is red.

The bed is big.

The man is hot.

The ant sat.

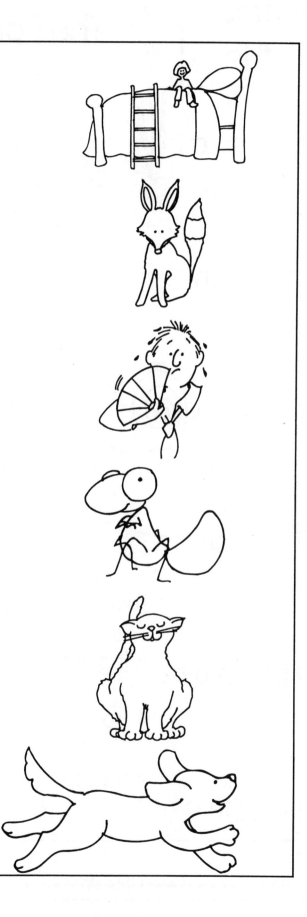

This is a big pond.

A log is in the pond.

A frog is on the log.

Jump, frog, jump.

I read this story to_____.

Reading

Draw:

frog	log

Fill in:

The pond is _____ .

A _____ is in the pond.

A _____ is on the log.

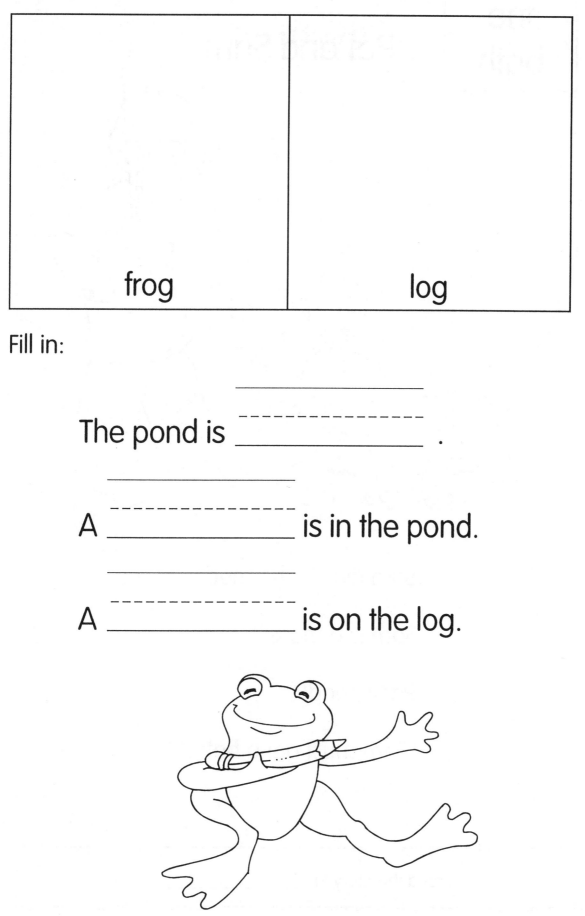

the
bath

Pat and Sam

Sam digs in the mud.

Sam is a mess.

Pat is mad!

"Sam must get a bath."

I read this story to_____.

Match:

Pat

mud

bath

Sam

Sam digs in _____ .

Pat is _____ .

Sam must get a _____ .

What is in the box?

Bob had a box.

The box had a lid.

Bob set the box on the step.

What is in the box?

She
the

"Get the box, Jan."

Jan gets the box.

She can not see in it.

What is in the box?

Pick
What

"Pick up the lid, Jan."

What is in the box?

for
toy

A fox is in the box.

It is a toy fox.

The toy fox is for Jan.

I read this story to_____.

Answer Key

Please take time to go over the work your child has completed. Ask your child to explain what he/she has done. Praise both success and effort. If mistakes have been made, explain what the answer should have been and how to find it. Let your child know that mistakes are a part of learning. The time you spend with your child helps let him/her know you feel learning is important.

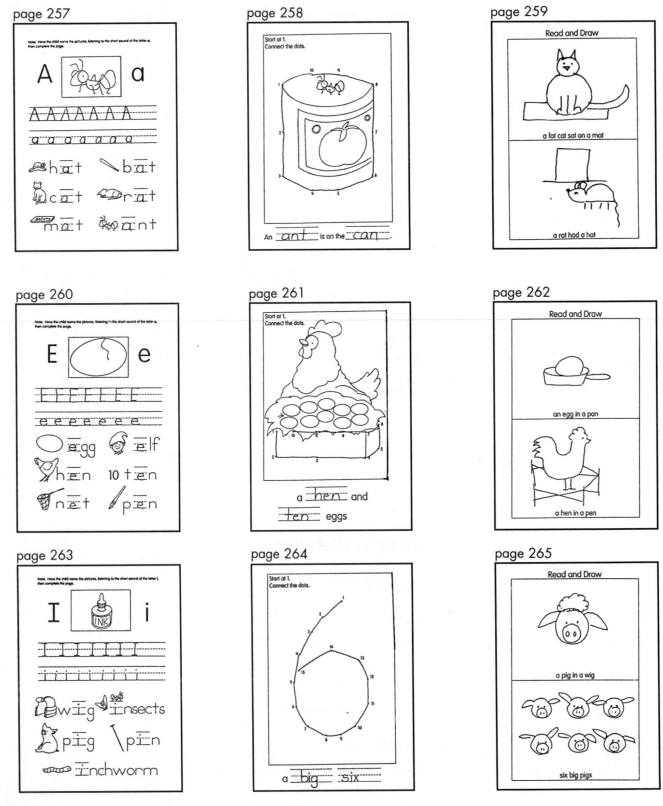

page 257

page 258

An ant is on the can.

page 259

Read and Draw

a fat cat sat on a mat

a rat had a hat

page 260

page 261

a hen and ten eggs

page 262

Read and Draw

an egg in a pan

a hen in a pen

page 263

page 264

a big six

page 265

Read and Draw

a pig in a wig

six big pigs

page 266

O   o

ŏx   bŏx

dŏg   tŏp

ŏtter   fŏx

page 267

Start at 1.
Connect the dots.

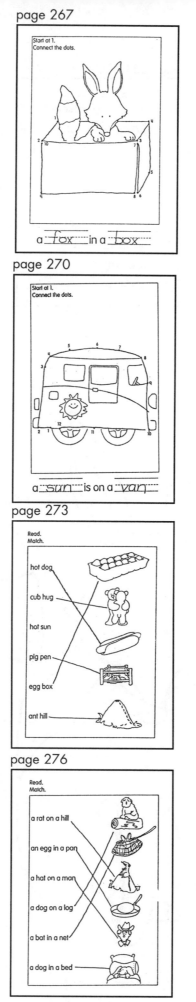

a fox in a box

page 268

Read and Draw

a dog on a log

a top in a box

page 269

Note: Have the child name the pictures, listening to the short sound of the letter u, then complete the page.

U   u

sŭn   bŭg

bŭs   ŭp

ŭmbrella

page 270

Start at 1.
Connect the dots.

a sun is on a van

page 271

Read and Draw

a nut is in a cup

a pup is in the mud

page 272

a e i o u

Match the vowel sounds.

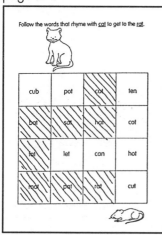

page 273

Read.
Match.

hot dog

cub hug

hot sun

pig pen

egg box

ant hill

page 274

Read and Draw

red
a big egg in the red box

black
a black hat on the man

a fat pig in the pen

page 275

Follow the words that rhyme with cat to get to the rat.

cub	pot	cot	ten
bat	sat	hat	cot
rat	let	can	hot
rat	pat	rat	cut

page 276

Read.
Match.

a rat on a hill

an egg in a pan

a hat on a man

a dog on a log

a bat in a net

a dog in a bed

Answers

page 277

Read.
Match.

The cat is fat.

The dog can run.

The fox is red.

The bed is big.

The man is hot.

The ant sat.

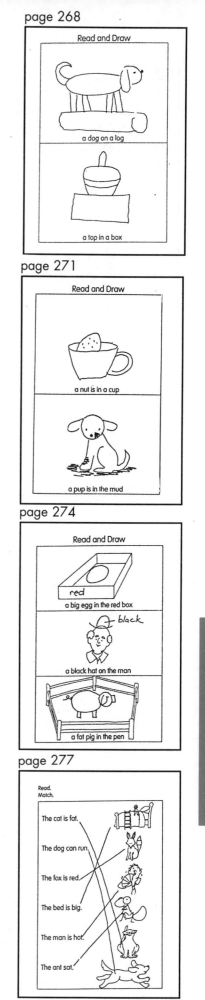

287

Short Vowels

page 279

page 281

Parents: Ask your child to show you how she/he can do each of the actions in the checklist below. Check the ones she/he does successfully.

Skill: has developed gross motor skills

☐ run

☐ skip

☐ hop *(one foot)*

☐ jump *(two feet)*

☐ walk along a line
(drawn in the dirt)

☐ catch a thrown object
*(something soft such as a
foam ball or a small pillow)*

Checking large motor skills

Parents: Ask your child to show you how she/he can do each of the actions in the checklist below. Check the ones she/he does successfully.

Skill: has developed fine motor skills

 ties a shoe lace into a bow

 closes a zipper

☐ buttons a piece of clothing

 closes a snap fastener

 fastens a Velcro® closing

☐ laces small objects onto a string *(spools, oat type cereal, beads, large buttons, etc.)*

Parents: Your child will need a crayon and a pencil to do pages 291 and 292.
Skill: can use a crayon and pencil to trace shapes

Start at the ★ .

Trace

Trace

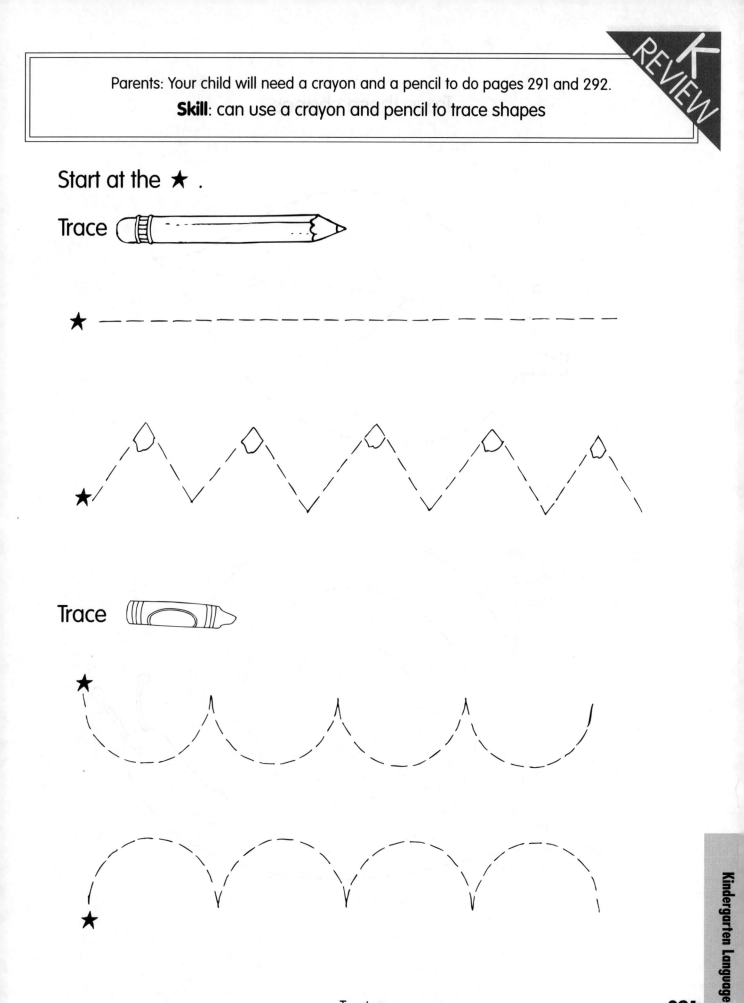

Trace these shapes.

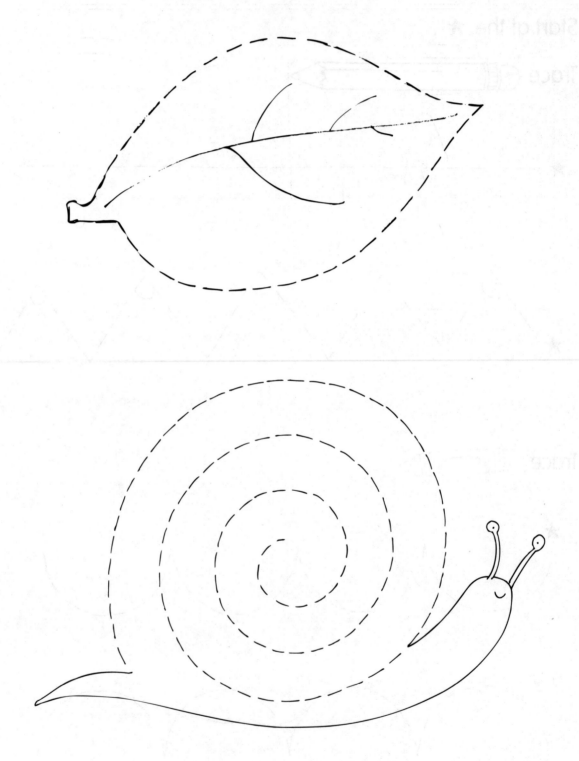

Parents: Your child will need a pair of scissors to do this page.
Supervise the activity if he/she is not experienced using scissors.

Skill: can use scissors to cut a specified shape

Using scissors

K

REVIEW

Parents: Your child will need a crayon or pencil to do this page.

Skill: demonstrates basic handwriting strokes

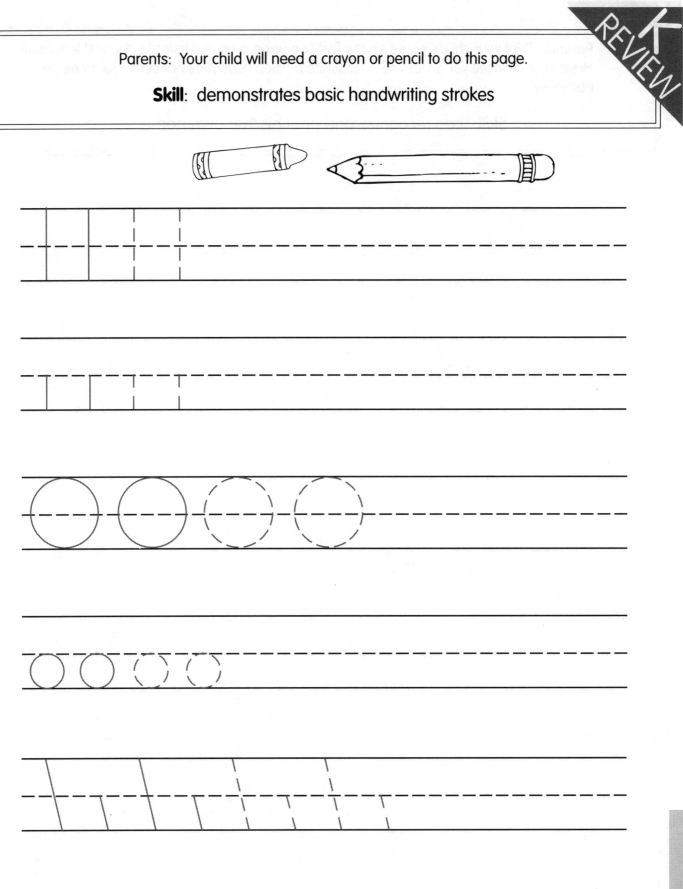

Parents: Print your child's name on the first line using a capital letter for the first letter only. Have your child tell you what you have written. Then have him/her copy the name on each line.

Skill: can recognize and print his/her own name

Printing my name

Parents: Follow the directions on this page to work with your child, then have him/her do page 298.

Skill: can recognize likenesses and differences in objects and pictures

Point to the first box on this page and ask the following series of questions.

"What do you see in this box?"
"What is the same about a ___(name the two objects)___?
"How are they different?"

Repeat the same three questions with the objects in all four boxes.

Comparing for likeness and difference

Skill: can recognize differences in objects and pictures

Put an X on the one that is different in each row.

Comparing for likeness and difference

Circle the ones that are the same in each row.

Match.

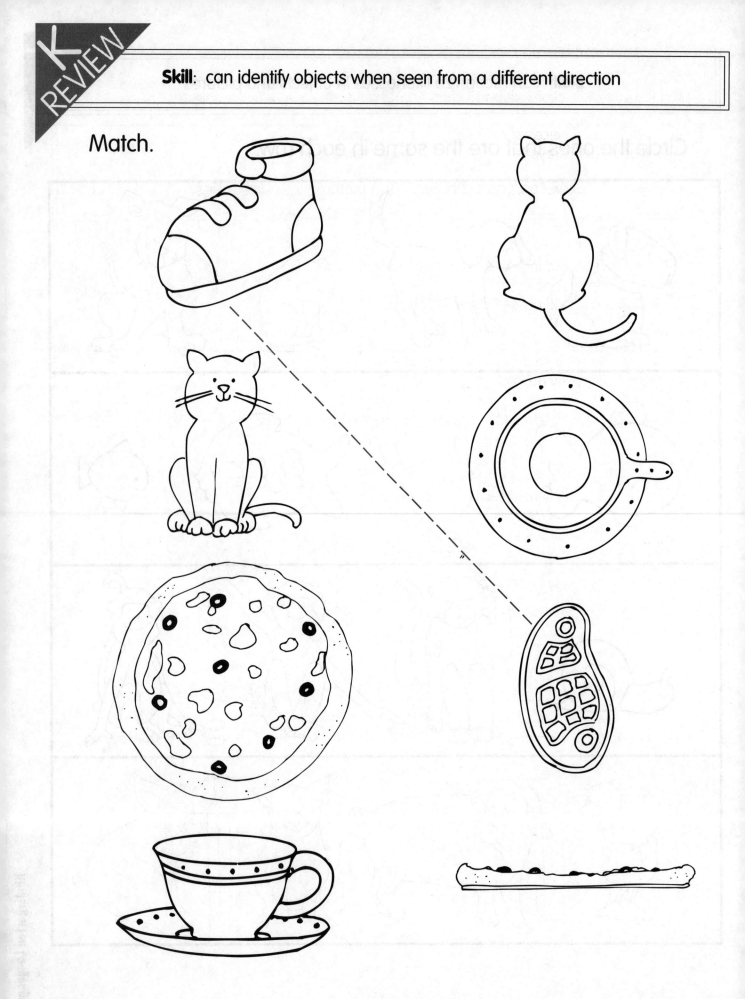

Matching

Parents: Collect these objects and place them where your child can reach them.
Then follow the directions below to check if your child can categorize the objects.

three small pieces of clothing   spoon, cup, small plate
pencil, pen, crayon   three food items

Skill: can group objects and pictures into categories

1.   Have your child look at all of the items on the table.
Have him/her name each item.
Help if the child doesn't know the name.

2.   Ask your child to pick three things that he/she thinks go together.
Then ask "Why do these go together?"

        Acceptable answers can be the obvious ones:
            Clothing - "We wear them."
            Food - "We eat them."

        Other answers might be less obvious:
        Writing items - "They all have points."
        Clothing - "They are made of cloth."
        Sock, apple, crayon - "They are red."

3.   Have your child do the job on page 302.

Classifying objects and pictures

Kindergarten Language

Skill: can group objects and pictures into categories

Color the pictures that go together.
Put an X on the picture that does not.

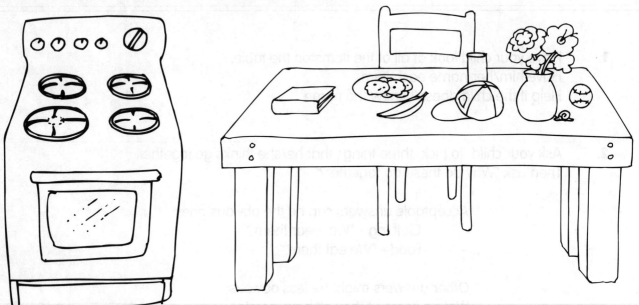

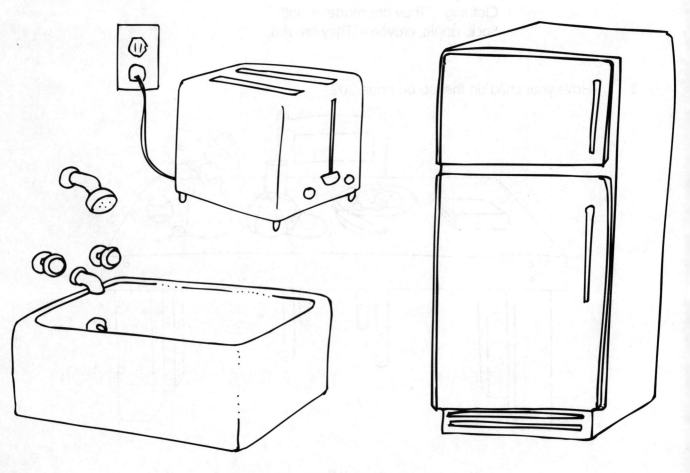

Classifying objects and pictures

Parents: Point to each letter and ask your child to give its name.
Circle the ones he/she can name

Skill: recognizes and can name the letters of the alphabet

a   b   c   d   e   f   g

h   i   j   k   l   m   n

o   p   q   r   s   t   u

v   w   x   y   z

I know _____ letters of the alphabet!
_{number}

Understanding alphabetic order   **303**

Skill: recognizes the difference between capital and lower case letters

Match the letters:

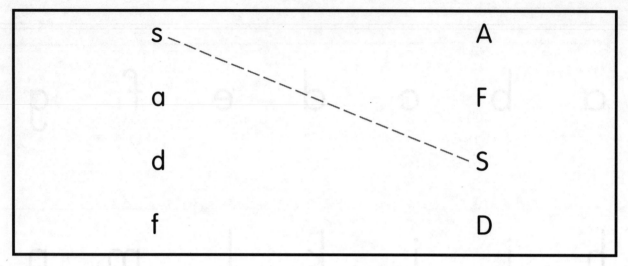

s   A

a   F

d   S

f   D

i   G

g   H

h   N

n   I

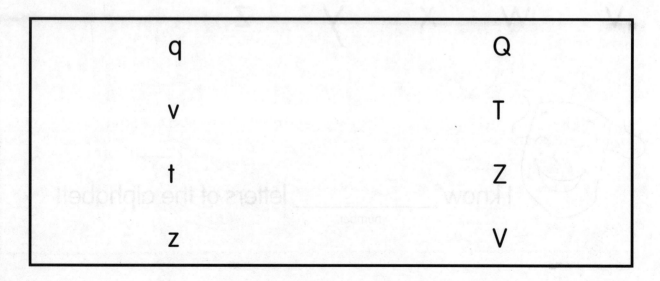

q   Q

v   T

t   Z

z   V

Matching lower case and capital letters

Parents: Ask your child to describe what he/she sees in this picture.

Skill: can describe the contents of a picture

Understanding picture details

Parents: Have your child look at each set of pictures.
Ask him/her to tell you what will happen next.
Accept any reasonable answer as correct.

Skill: can draw conclusions about what happens next

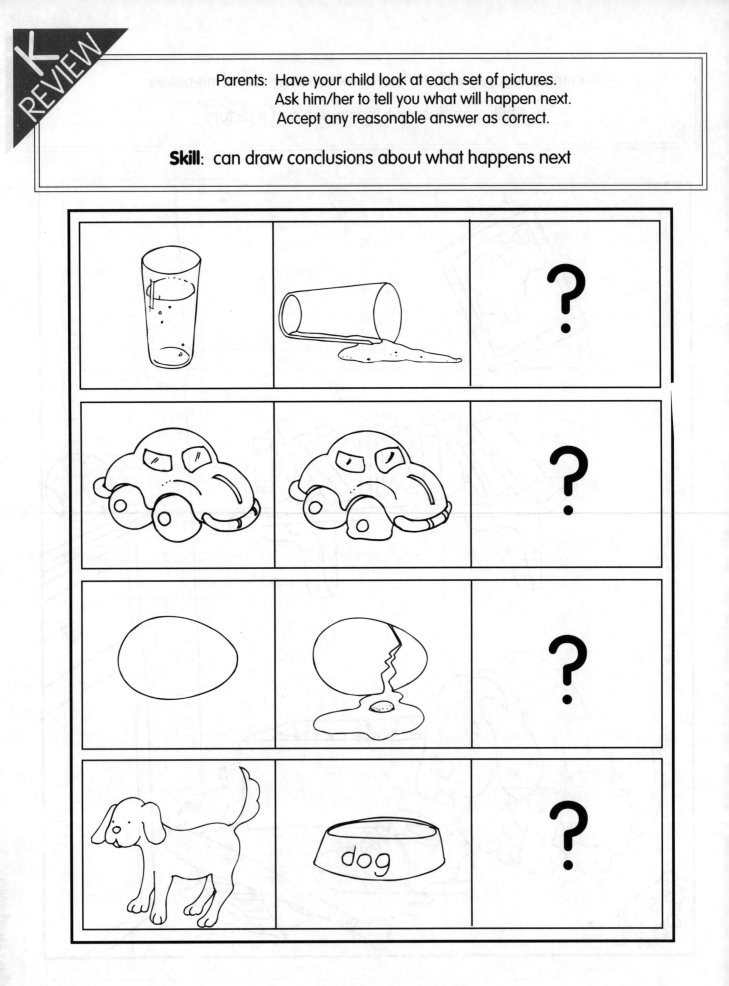

Parents: Your child will need scissors and paste or glue in order to do this page. Have your child cut the pictures apart and paste them in the boxes in the correct order.

Skill: can sequence pictures in correct order

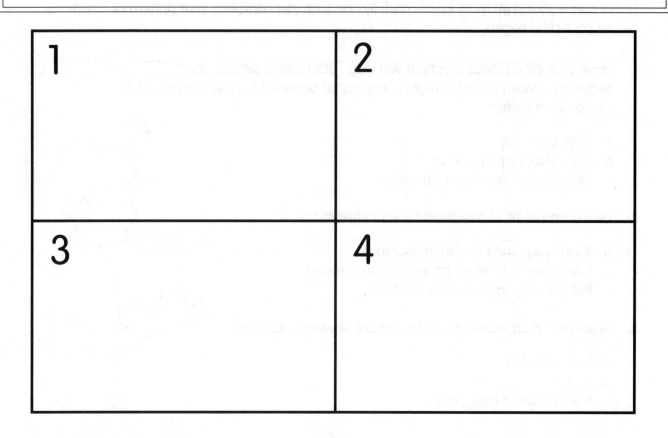

Parents: Follow the directions below to check your child's listening skills.

Skill: has developed good listening skills

In this game your child must listen carefully. Be sure you complete your pattern or directions before your child begins.

1. Have your child repeat a pattern you clap. Start with a simple, short sequence. Make a longer, more complicated pattern if he/she is successful at the short pattern.

   a. clap, clap, clap
   b. clap, clap, clap-clap-clap
   c. clap, clap, snap, clap, clap, snap

2. Give a simple list of directions for your child to follow.

   a. Touch your head and then your toes.
   b. Stamp your feet three times and turn around.
   c. Put your left hand on your right ear.

3. Have your child repeat a list of numbers or words after you.

   a. bee, baa, boo
   b. 2, 4, 6
   c. Katy caught a kangaroo.

Parents: Read the directions one at a time for your child.
Have him/her mark the correct answer.

Skill: can listen to follow oral directions

1. Put an X on the animal that says "Moo."

2. Put a circle around the animal that swims in the water.

3. Put a line under the animal that can climb a tree.

4. Color the animal that lays eggs.

Listening to follow directions

Parents: Read this story to your child, then ask him/her to tell you the answers to the questions listed below.

Skill: can listen to a story, then answer questions about it

Kelly's Kitten

When Kelly left the kitchen, she thought her kitten Stan was asleep. Boy, was she wrong! As soon as she left, that naughty kitten went racing across the kitchen. He jumped up on the counter and began to look for something to play with.

Stan saw a basket on a shelf in the corner. He loved to climb into baskets. He gave a big jump and landed on the shelf. Oh, no! The shelf began to move. Down fell the basket and down fell Stan.

"Maybe I'll just find something to eat," thought Stan. He was a very smart kitten. He knew the cat food was in the cupboard by the refrigerator. He pulled at the cupboard door until it came open. He climbed into the cupboard and found the bag of food. He tore a hole in the side of the bag and began to gobble up the tasty cat food.

Stan was so busy eating, he didn't hear Kelly come back into the kitchen. Now Stan has to sleep in the laundry room and the cat food has been moved to the top shelf of the cupboard.

1. Who is Kelly?   (Kelly was a little girl.)

2. Who is Stan?   (Stan was Kelly's kitten.)

3. How do you know Stan is a smart kitten?
   (He knew where the cat food was; he could open cupboard doors.)

4. What happened first - Stan ate cat food or Stan tried to get into the basket?
   (He tired to get into the basket.)

5. What happened when Kelly saw Stan eating the cat food?
   (She put him in the laundry room to sleep and she moved the cat food.)

REVIEW K

Parents: Have our child draw a picture of himself/herself at play, then tell you what he/she looks like. Listen for words that describe color, size, actions, feelings, etc.

Skill: can describe his/herself using correct vocabulary

This is _____ .
child's name

Describing

Kindergarten Language

311

Parents: Read these rhymes to your child one at a time. Ask him/her to tell you which words sound the same (rhyme). Repeat the rhyme if your child needs to hear it again.

Skill: recognizes rhythm and rhyme

1. Jack and Jill
went up a hill.
(Jill and hill)

2. Little Miss Muffet
Sat on a tuffet.
(Muffet, tuffet)

3. A little bat sat on my hat.
(bat, sat, hat)

4. The funny clown fell down.
(clown, down)

K REVIEW

Color pictures that rhyme.
X pictures that do not rhyme.

bat

cat

hen

car

box

jar

sock

frog

dog

Skill: recognizes and identifies colors

Parents:

1. Get a box of crayons. Show each of the following colors to your child and ask him/her to tell you its name.

   red   yellow   blue
   green   orange   black
   white   brown   purple

2. Lay the crayons out and ask your child to hand you the one you name.

3. Now go on a "color hunt" with your child throughout the house.
   In each room have him/her try to find something that has the colors you named.

Parents: Have your child draw one thing he/she found on the color hunt for each color listed. Read the color names to your child if necessary.

Let's Go On a Color Hunt

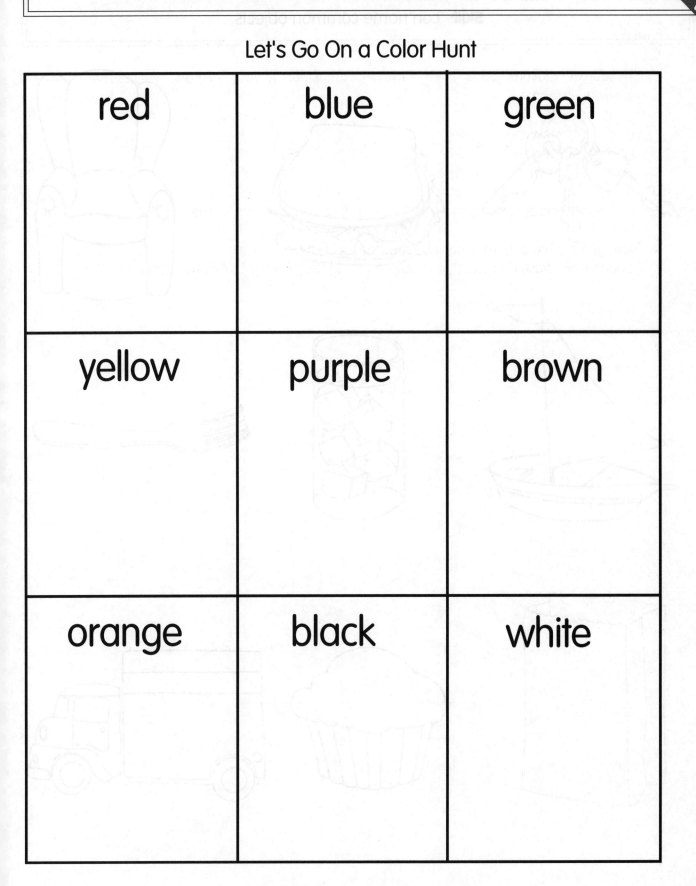

red	blue	green
yellow	purple	brown
orange	black	white

Recognizing color words and colors

Parents: Point to the objects on page 316 and 317 one at a time. Ask your child to tell you the name of each object.

Skill: can name common objects

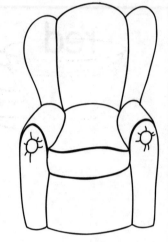

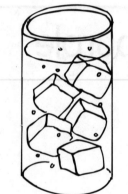

Identifying the names of common objects

Parents: Point to each picture and ask your child to describe what is happening.

Skill: can describe the action taking place in a picture

Describing actions

Parents: The best way to tell if your child has developed good language skills is to listen as he/she talks to you and with others. Observe your child over a period of time and check the skills he/she does well.

Skills: has developed language well enough to communicate with others

☐ can tell about his/her own experiences

☐ can express what he/she needs or wants

☐ asks questions

☐ understands what others are trying to communicate

☐ speaks in complete sentences most of the time

☐ can retell a familiar story

☐ can repeat verses from memory

You can encourage good language development by talking to your child, explaining what is going on and naming objects in the environment. Another excellent way to encourage language growth is to read to your child on a regular basis.

Communicating with others

Answer Key

Please take time to go over the work your child has completed. Ask your child to explain what he/she has done. Praise both success and effort. If mistakes have been made, explain what the answer should have been and how to find it. Let your child know that mistakes are a part of learning. The time you spend with your child helps let him/her know you feel learning is important.

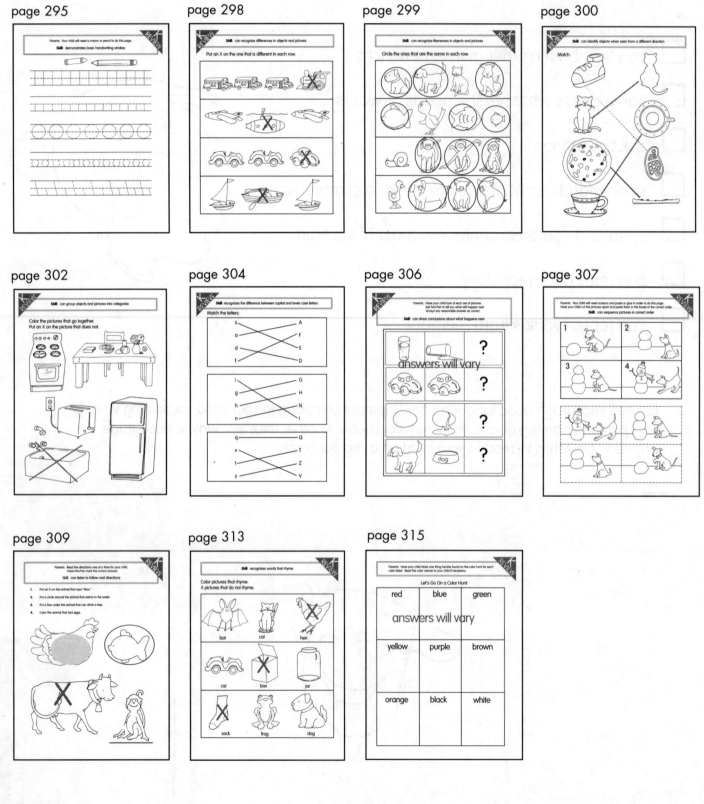

page 295

page 298

page 299

page 300

page 302

page 304

page 306

page 307

page 309

page 313

page 315